The 'Confe Hayling Rescue

By Frank Dunster

3rd edition May 2014

Edited by Tony Aitken

Introduction

Tony Aitken

May 20th 2014

'Hayling Rescue' is an aluminum hulled RIB, built in Chichester Harbour by Pepe's Boatyard. The orange RIB is a familiar sight to most sailors, fishermen, yachtsmen, dinghy sailors, windsurfers, paddle boarders, canoeists and rowers, who use and enjoy the wonderful waters of Chichester Harbour. Hayling Rescue's Skipper is Frank Dunster, a native of Hayling Island, Hampshire, on the South Coast of England.

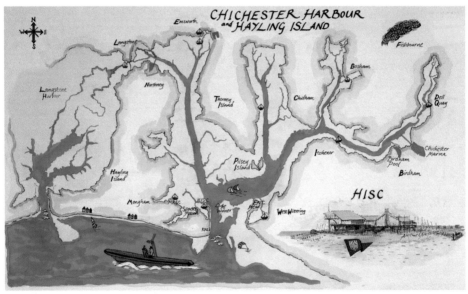

To help with orientation, though not with navigation, this map of the waters around Hayling Island will hopefully assist you to figure out where some of the places referred to in 'The Confessions' are situated.

You can never have too many friends! There is the Facebook 'Friends of Hayling Rescue' group from where these pages are gathered, and there is the well established fund raising 'Friends of Hayling Rescue' group.

Frank's musings and comments on life as Hayling Rescue over the past two years are collected here. In the slightly anarchic way of running a project such as this, it is assumed that as an open group, the Facebook FoHR are happy to allow their names and nick-names to be referenced, even occasionally taken in vain, but all of course, in the best possible taste, and in a very good cause.

For those unfamiliar with the Facebook social networking site, it uses postings, comments, photos, and of course 'likes', and these can all be made by any member of a Group, and are seen by all members who look at the Group page. Private messages can be sent to other Group members, so all in all it is a pretty useful piece of 'cloud' software.

Postings are made in date order, so for this compilation, everything had to be reversed, the first shall be last, from 2011 to date of final edit. The follow up comments from group members have not been included, only original postings. The references to 'Over to you Tone' and the like, are gentle hints that perhaps a YouTube clip of some pertinent piece of music, TV, or film extract, might be appropriate, and a few are included to give you an idea. The actual links are all on the Group site at the time of writing, so if you go to the FoHR FB Group you can enjoy the comments on Frank's posts, and hopefully be surprised at the inventiveness of some of the suggestions, music, and other links.

You will notice many abbreviations, for example: Chi Har for Chichester Harbour, and HISC for Hayling Island Sailing Club. There are many more and hopefully you will soon puzzle your way through all but the most obscure of references. The spelling and punctuation in many of the posts is not perfect, many were uploaded from mobile phones or tablets, often from the water. You will surely forgive, and I trust enjoy the informal and occasionally inventive style of the Author's jottings.

These are remarkable thoughts from a remarkable man, and well worth preserving. They truly are some of the most original and witty observations ever to be written about life on the water between The Chichester Bar, My Lord's Pond, and Fernando's hideaway.

Carry on…!

Frank aka Hayling Rescue, on the balcony of Hayling Island Sailing Club aka HISC. West Wittering in the background.

Chris Bashall

August 30, 2011

I had the pleasure of being rescued by Frank yesterday.
I managed to get caught out by the speed of the huge tides whilst having a picnic on Easthead with friends. I had moored the rib well away from the beach in waist deep water and used the inflatable to get us ashore. the tide turned and started ebbing. I had noticed that the rib had stopped bobbing up and down and figured the outboard leg had touched down, so I waded out to find the rib had just touched down, so I lifted the motor and walked it out back into waist deep water and re anchored. I walked back to the beach and within 5 minutes it had stopped bobbing again, I waded back out to find the hull was already sitting on the bottom in shin deep water! This time I had left the leg up and the tide was literally ripping out almost as quickly as I could walk. I shouted to the friends to round everything up and get out asap to give me a hand drag the rib into deeper water. By the time they arrived it was too late. The water had gone from 3' deep to just covering my toes within 5 minutes!!
I called Hayling Rescue for assistance in the hope Frank might have been able to tow it through the silt back into deeper water, but he did a couple of test pulls using an anchor to gauge how much thrust he could generate and declared that the tidal flow was too strong. So we ferried everyone out with the inflatable to Franks rib and he gave us a lift back to the club. He then kindly ran me back out

4

at around midnight to retrieve the rib once we had some water again.
What a fantastic service Frank offers, you really don't realize just what a
valuable resource he is, until you need his assistance.
Apart from my pathetic problems, having dropped us off he went off to another
similar incident and then onto a paddle boarder who had slipped off in shallow
water and had managed to break his ankle, they apparently floated him on his
board into the back of Frank's open transom and rushed him off for medical
assistance. It never stops for Frank.

Chris Bashall added Hayling Rescue to the group.

November 22, 2011

Hayling Rescue

February 24, 2012

Hayling Rescue in 2011 took part in 212 rescue incidents as well as all the
commercial work. these incidents involved 4 sinking boats the righting of 44
capsized dinghies pulling 31 grounded yachts into deeper water rescuing 12
windsurfers diving underneath 16 yachts to clear fouled propellers towing home
38 boats with engine failure 2 boats on fire first aid rendered on 3 occasions and
a host of other incidents. Sadly I have to admit that it was just a typical year

Hayling Rescue

April 18, 2012

Hayling Rescue was in action overnight on behalf of Seastart who had a
member with a 33 foot ketch at anchor at East Head with a flat battery. The
engine restarted immediately with jump start kit the anchor was raised and the
yacht motored off in the darkness to Chi Marina. Frank returned to a sheltered
mooring off seagull island to resume his slumbers

Hayling Rescue

April 19, 2012

Our best wishes go to Pete Hanscombe and Hannah who get married on
Saturday the 21st of April. Peter was a superb crew on Hayling Rescue from
2006 onward and played his role as rescue swimmer with great relish, as
Thelma will testify. Peter now works full time for the RNLI and has recently
qualified as a deputy staff coxswain at Spurn Point Humber.

Hayling Rescue

April 20, 2012

Hayling Rescue had a relatively quiet end to the week with incidents which included diving underneath a motor cruiser in Sparkes Marina to cut off a rope from around its propeller advising a lost mariner how to get up Mill Rythe and then attending a 40ft catamaran which had a small tear in its starboard hull and was taking on water. A portable electric pump was set up until the vessel could be lifted out at Emsworth

Chris Bashall

April 22, 2012

Frank told us life is absurd, Saturday evening he was off to Pete Hanscombe's wedding reception and got as far as crabbers bridge when a lone sailor in his 75 foot motor cruiser called on the VHF to the coastguard for assistance after cutting his hand badly while re-anchoring his boat during one of the squalls and being blown onto the Nutbourne Marshes, Frank in his Sunday best returned to the club leapt on Hayling Rescue and arrived on the scene 5 minutes later together with chi har patrol. the man was evacuated to St. Richard's hospital. On their return frank still in smartly pressed trousers and posh sweater helped the Harbour master pull the vessel off the mudbank to a deep water anchorage nearby. The motor yacht weighed 80 tons had three stories an engine room the size of hisc members bar and all modern conveniences excluding a jacuzzi. Frank now having missed the reception returned to HISC still in Sunday best, and finding local shops closed, raided the club vending machine for his supper..... cheese and onion crisps and a packet of Revels.

How the rich live!

Hayling Rescue

May 3, 2012

Hayling Rescue will be craned out at Sparkes Marina on Monday May 14th for its annual overhaul.....nearly two years since it's last one.... Mike and Dean Frith's paint division will be stripping back the 24 coats of anti-fouling applied to the hull in the last 12 years and putting on fresh protection as currently we are down 7 knots on top speed.....also the engineer from Hamilton Jets will strip down the water jet drive and replace or repair where necessary....after 12 busy years it deserves it.. these three items will be funded by the fund raising quorate of the FRIENDS who already have the cash in the bank plus a bit over for the routine engine maintenance schedule undertaken by Golden Arrow Marine in July and December this year. Frank will also be doing and funding other items on this refit in order to keep the boat in tiptop condition after 12 busy years since new. Hayling Rescue should be relaunched in time for the major charity race the Glyn Charles pursuit on Sunday 20th May. Hayling Rescue wishes to express grateful thanks to all who have helped keep the service going...........Merry Christmas.

Hayling Rescue

May 12, 2012

Why does he always carry that damn radio? Frank was in the inner sanctum of HISC having just had three cups of HISC coffee when that damn radio crackled annoyingly in the wash basin. Frank dashed outside to hear a motorboat sending out a mayday call reporting being unable to recover two persons from a sunken dinghy somewhere in Chi Harbour. Frank nipped down to his boat and joined up with the harbour patrol at Channel and assisted with the recovery of the people. And more fool him, because he was wearing a wetsuit, entered the sea to help recover the semi-submerged Wayfarer. All was well and all returned to Northney Marina. The Wayfarer had capsized by a heavy gust just as the owner opened the stern hatch....also because the crew were wearing automatic inflatable life jackets the person in the motor boat could not pull them onboard......Frank admitted to one other embarrassing radio call when he was in the shower in Sparkes Marina on a stormy day. The coastguard who had called him up for assistance in some drama at sea thought he was already on scene.

Chris Bashall

May 13, 2012

Introducing the fabulous House of Dunster 2012 Summer Collection, featuring

Frank in his eye catching woolly hat and several layers beneath the dry suit. We are told that the next release from the House of Dunster will be the new ultra skimpy, transparent when wet shorts range, complete with mosquito net!

Haylng Rescue

May 21, 2012

For Peter, speed is back to 30 knots.......A relatively quiet weekend...An old gaff rigged yacht towed into Sparkes. in the excitement of the sail they forgot the diesel. Scottie's ashes were scattered with full ecclesiastical and military honours and the sailing for the Glyn Charles memorial trophy was to a high standard with over a hundred boats and very few capsizes Katie and Colin in 'Piglet' gave a few anxious moments to the rock stars, but James Peters was unphased to take the honours. Jerry Keller is coming good but watch out for brisk easterlies at the weekend......hail sign Hayling Rescue.

Hayling Rescue

May 23, 2012

Question...What happens when you are an elderly yachtsman enjoying a sunny sail?
In a nice north westerly breeze and you reach the Harbour entrance and all of a sudden a brisk south westerly sea breeze sets in.......well you go round and round in circles and then when your engine does not start you panic.....after 2 panicky mobile phone calls to ea start and the Harbour office muggins is duly dispatched and the yacht is taken in tow for the Itchenor moorings....just then another yacht sends out a mayday call on the vhf radio....

"Am sinking in Hayling Bay"....

Fortunately 3 other vessels are in the area and the Hayling and Portsmouth Lifeboats are launched to assist....then after returning the first yacht to its mooring muggins has to go to Thornham Marina to pick up a yacht to return to its mooring in Emsworth Harbour only there is not enough tide to float the yacht out of the Thornham Pool. I think the season has just truly started........roll on family fun week.

HR on mark laying duty.

Hayling Rescue

May 27, 2012

No sooner had basher Bashall redone the electrics on 3 of Hayling Rescue's bilge pumps then we were off for the usual Saturday mayhem. 3 windsurfer incidents later and a broken down motor cruiser needed a tow back to Chichester Marina..........These tow you home incidents are never straight forward and a sunny day turns into a family nightmare with sea sick kids and all the rest. Still I did enjoy seeing the Chichester Cathedral Spire in the evening sun and got back in time to make the shops for my usual supper of a large Cadbury's Dairy Milk washed down with a carton of orange juice. Their ain't no cure for the summertime blues.

Hayling Rescue

May 25, 2012

One of Hayling Rescue's main incident categories is "engine failures" and on Thursday two separate incidents involved towing a yacht with an overheating engine into Northney Marina and a motor boat into Sparkes with a complete engine failure. 4 rescue incidents in 4 days makes me wonder if we will be handling over 200 incidents for the second year in a row.......and we still have family fun week to look forward to....roll out those lazy hazy crazy days of summer......thank you Nat King Cole.

Hayling Rescue

May 26, 2012

I bet the lazy b..... sits in the sun all day.. despite my best intentions it was not to be as Friday saw another rescue incident. this time Hayling Rescue was dispatched by sea start to a yacht in the Thorney Channel with a major problem with its propeller and had just managed to sail back to its mooring. Jacques Cousteau dived underneath to clear a clump of seaweed entangled around the saildrive unit. The request to tow a yacht from Stokes Bay to Mill Rythe was politely declined and preparations were made for a busy weekend... now where did I hide that deckchair?....What was the name of that song by Eddie Cochran?

Hayling Rescue

June 4, 2012

Frank has been blessed with some superb crew in the 2000s Ian puffer Williams, Neil 'Digger' Driscoll, Ben 'Sarge Popham and 'Portacabin' Pete Hanscombe. All have moved on to bigger and better things. consequently Frank is seeking an energetic crew member to help with the many rescue incidents. Hayling Rescue, while using the traditional techniques, likes to deploy a rescue swimmer who can help right a capsized dinghy quickly dive underneath to push back in a dagger board or rescue a trapped person and skilled enough to sail the dinghy home if needs be.there will be numerous other incidents to attend and the candidate will not mind being wet and cold and have developed a sense of humour to cope with a gale of wind on Chichester bar, Federation week and family fun week. there is of course no pay although you may be eligible for tea and cakes after racing and perhaps a cucumber sandwich on regatta day. there will be opportunities to learn emergency first aid and RYA advanced powerboating. This is a serious ad and hopefully you will enjoy it all enough to go on to bigger and better things with your sense of humour intact and an appreciation of quality cuisine.

Hayling Rescue

June 8, 2012

Hayling Rescue has had a real stinker of a day mainly recovering yachts broken away from their moorings all over the harbour where there has been winds gusting up to 50 knots for most of the day. Will Thompson and Dave Nicholls kindly came on board to lend a hand and were quite superb in helping sort out the various dramas. i am still hopefull we will have a summer and some quieter times but am running out of summer songs to help with the narratives..............
Mungo Jerry......... 'In the Summertime when the weather is fine.........'

Hayling Rescue

June 10, 2012

St. Swithin's day is not until the middle of July and the secret is that if it rains on that day it will rain for the next 40 days as a south westerly airstream has set in and usually does not clear until the first easterly blow of September that is why family fun week is so much fun. Hayling Rescue is hopeful that this current bad weather will clear during the week beginning June 18th as various people are holding birthday barbecues on east head on Saturday the 23rd...... however the law of averages comes into play and we must have some sun soon to make this the usual average summer. ....summer nights by Marianne Faithful is relevant in this respect and it may have been penned by Jagger and Richards, Google it someone…

Hayling Rescue

June 16, 2012

Very many congratulations to Jamie and Sarah....Frank will probably not turn up for his own wedding and reception let alone his funeral....things started happening around high noon with a windsurfer with broken gear on the winner bank and then various problems were sorted out on the moorings followed by a motor cruiser aground... on the Winner Bank then a trip to Warblington to set up the recovery of a Westerly Consort broken away from the Langstone moorings.....Frank then returned to float the yacht off its mudbank and into Northney marina on top of the tide returning th hisc at ten of the clock pm. having missed the festivities Frank toasted the good health of the bride and groom with a packet of revels from the club vending machine washed down with a carton of guava juice.... many thanks are due to golden arrow marine for their speedy repair.........Hayling Rescue wishes everyone a peaceful and joyful sunny summer when it arrives.......and that includes family fun week.

Hayling Rescue

June 15, 2012

Hayling Rescue lives....following the dramas of the past few weeks Hayling Rescue developed a major engine cooling water leak... a blown head gasket was feared..... golden arrow marine duly attended and discovered a major failure of the heat exchanger it was not repairable so a new one was ordered and fitted on friday........fortunately the financial 'Friends of Hayling Rescue' had sufficient funds in the contingency reserve fund to pay this expense.......let us hope we have a quieter summer but we have rs feva worlds family fun week federation week and all the other events in the Harbour coming up shortly plus strong winds forecast for tomorrow................ the Kinks come to mind.. 'Lazing on a sunny afternoon.. in the summertime....'' Merry Christmas.

Hayling Rescue

June 25, 2012

The Great Escape is on......or what is that song about mondays......

Having had a quiet cup of coffee on the HISC balcony with the bishop in the morning sunshine as all was quiet and tranquil Hayling Rescue was thinking of catching up on lost sleep. vhf radio came to life with a mayday call from 'The Great Escape', an 18 foot angling boat, taking in water and sinking on the approaches to Chi Harbour ...the snooze was postponed and Hayling Rescue proceeded to the chi bar to assist. the vessel was taking water fast but was saved by one of the crew bailing 20 to the dozen with a large bucket. He was on leave from the army in Afghanistan and had decided that as he had eluded the Taliban, Davy Jones was not going to take him on his homecoming fishing trip treat. thus the vessel was beached at Eaststoke Point and the owner taken to Northney Marina to collect car and trailer. The vessel was eventually recovered from the HISC slipway courtesy of the Harbour patrol.... it seems the vessel had a 2 foot split in the chine along the bow from hitting one of the usual bar seas we are often greeted with.......So no snooze... And maybe not until next Monday as there appears to be events happening every day this week. 'Monday Monday can't trust that day.......'

Hayling Rescue

June 25, 2012

Sometimes weekends are drama free. The HISC Opi weekend was well run and the rescue fleet coped well in the conditions. Thus Hayling Rescue stayed mainly on the pontoon. A quiet night was anticipated at long last as the wind eventually eased to allow Frank a peaceful night's sleep on the approaches to My Lord's Pond...........However slumbers were interrupted mid evening by the Coastguard who had a 999 call reporting a yacht drifting down the Harbour on the tide. Frank removed himself from warm sleeping bag and joined roger of the Harbour Patrol alongside the yacht in gallon reach. the owner had been below deck cooking supper and had not noticed his anchor not holding. Frank returned to his slumbers somewhat alarmed at how eerily quiet the evening had become. what on earth was going on. all was revealed when frank was awoken yet again by a text message from D.T. in Hong Kong now no longer an England supporter and vowing to boycott spag. bol. this was followed by the wailing of sirens from the local fire engine and then the seagulls opened up in protest. sleep was eventually attained around midnight. I wonder what the new week will bring..... round the island race next saturday..... RS Feva worlds ... family fun week bring on fed week..... roll out those lazy hazy crazy days of summer.

HR tows a stricken motor boat to safety.

Hayling Rescue

July 7, 2012

We can cast another veil on this weekend's summer activities with Hayling Rescue needing to put the roof up again in the bedroom..... however we can savor another musical delight if Tony Aitken can come up with…

The Mamas & The Papas - 'Monday Monday'

Hayling Rescue

June 28, 2012

What was that about London buses?...

Sparkes Marina called on Hayling Rescue's services to tow in a yacht just outside the marina with an engine failure due to a flat battery.........then during the tow a rigid hulled inflatable called up for a tow into the marina due to an engine failure due to...........a flat battery......still it has been a productive week with golden arrow marine doing a 400 hour engine service which should see Hayling Rescue through RS Feva worlds family fun week junior racing week federation week rs 800 and 600 nationals and all the other Chichester Harbour activities. 'Oh, its a long long time from May to September.......'.

Hayling Rescue

July 2, 2012

Hayling Rescue had a relatively quiet weekend, just an RS 200 with a broken mast off west wittering,a motor boat with a rope around the propeller cleared by mask and snorkel, an X boat aground on the stocker sands and an RS Vision towed in in blustery winds.......Still no settled weather so an opportunity for Tony Aitken to give us some Carol King…

Carole King - 'It Might As Well Rain Until September' - 1962

Hayling Rescue

July 11, 2012

What we need Tony is a montage of Here Comes Summer'...Jerry Keller… V.A.C.A.T.I.O.N…Connie Francis...'Lazy Hazy Crazy Days of Summer'…Nat King Cole and 'Schools Out.'..Alice Cooper…

'Summertime Blues' - The Who Live at the Isle of Wight

Hayling Rescue

July 13, 2012

It had been a long week and Friday saw basher Bashall come down to sort out a small leak on the water jet units hydraulics. nutrition had not been high on the list either so when rack of lamb was spotted on the club dinner menu a decent meal beckoned at long last as Hayling Rescue walked in to claim the feast the mobile phone came to life it was HM Coastguard and would I mind very much in helping them out by towing a small speedboat with an engine failure back to itchenor........ An hour later it was back to the club vending machine for yet another evening meal of a packet of crisps and the chocolate revels........ Oh well there is always the club breakfast to look forward to tomorrow morning.............The condemned ate a hearty meal..........Merry Christmas one and all…

Oliver! The Musical. 'Food Glorious Food'

HR tows home another stricken craft.

Hayling Rescue

July 18, 2012

Hayling Rescue was reflecting on the lack of action......not even someone with a rope around the propellor........the phone rang

"Remember me? You kindly got my mooring chain off when it was wrapped around my propeller last year.... Well I was coming along to my mooring when......."

Ten minutes later Jacques Cousteau was again in action underneath a yacht up some back creek. fortunately after a few attempts the errant chain was untangled from the propeller and put around the mooring cleat...... and then it started to rain again. but cheer up, after Saturday we are assured of a sunny week just in time for the RS Feva worlds and DT and family's annual visit from Hong Kong.......... up the Villa...

Mamas and Papas 'Creque Alley'

Hayling Rescue

July 18, 2012

XC weather for Hayling Island has it that the weather comes good late Friday and Saturday then an easterly sets in by Wednesday so we must move on to the more positive summer songs......So Tony we must start off with beach baby from your magic jukebox followed by Beach Boys 'Do it Again'.

Hayling Rescue

July 24, 2012

Hayling Rescue had a quiet weekend with only one rescue of note to a 28 foot yacht in Hayling Bay which had its spinnaker sheet and spinnaker wrapped around its propeller. the skippers wife had endeavored to free it but had had to be hauled back on board with the help of a passing yacht when she got cold and tired.. thus Jacques Cousteau was in action again although being a bit of a sissy he changed out of the 3mm summer steamer into the 6mm wet suit. the rope was untangled from around the propeller and the spinnaker recovered and the yacht was sent on its way rejoicing. we tactfully refrained from asking the skipper why he deployed his spinnaker with the engine still running...........This was the third time in 5 days that Jacques Cousteau had been in action.....now just where did I store that old 8mm wet suit.............I will leave it to Tony's magic jukebox to supply an appropriate accompaniment...

'Dive! Dive! Dive!' Bruce Dickinson.

Hayling Rescue

July 28, 2012

With the RS Feva worlds being particularly well organised and marshalled and with the sparkling weather Hayling Rescue had a quiet week. A neaped yacht needed a hefty pull off a mudbank at Sweare Deep and there were two vessels with flat batteries in the Bosham Harbour. Jacques Cousteau was again in action clearing a massive growth of worm like barnacles on the propeller of a Halberg Rassy 34 which was about to embark on a cruise and had no drive from the encrusted drive unit. A 36 foot Bavaria yacht took the safe anchorage at east head too literally and found itself aground at ......high tide.... With Hayling Rescue healing the yacht over on its side from the masthead the Harbour patrol launch pulled the sailing school yacht into deep water to the cheers of the people on other anchored yachts......... Or were they cheering the plight of the Instructor and his errant pupils? Oh well life goes on and perhaps Tony and his magic jukebox can come up with an appropriate accompaniment to the text. Lead on Mcduff.

'Cheers' Theme 1983.

Hayling Rescue

July 29, 2012

I thought it might be one of those weekends when coffee on the balcony with the bishop was interrupted by the coastguard wanting Hayling Rescue tow a broken down motor boat just outside the harbour. as usual the vessel was off Langstone Harbour and so a long tow was taken to Chichester Marina then refueling was interrupted to tow in a laser on the bar with a broken mast then having refueled ...another 120 quid up the swanee..... I thought there was a recession?......then a call to an RS Vision with problems.Then Saturday evening was canceled when Sea Start wanted Hayling Rescue to tow a Sigma 33 with an engine failure back to its mooring at Itchenor. Supper then was 2 packets of nuts washed down with orange juice followed by a Cadbury's Dairy Milk... Smaller for the same price what recession....then Sunday breakfast was interrupted by a yacht aground on the winner bank... it got itself off then an RS100 had problems with an over slippery centre board then a laser 4000 was an encountered with a lady crew with a bang on the head from a boom then a couple of RS Fevas had problems near the tide gauge then a broken down speedboat was spotted on a lee shore near Thorney Island then a young windsurfer was given a lift ashore then a fast trip up the Emsworth channel was the order of the day to refloat a racing keel boat aground near vicar point then a trip to the canteen for an ice cream....a magnum....and a cup of coffee then to east head to a report of a rib with fuel problems which they had solved when Hayling Rescue appeared then a quick check over of the boat and gear and a telephone call to nat west computer banking to see if there is enough left of the overdraft for another 120 quids worth of diesel tomorrow morning........ this will be followed by a few hastily written invoices................but I did enjoy the icecream..... and tomorrow is family fun week........bliss.

Hayling Rescue

August 3, 2012

Forgive me for lapsing into the vernacular but it was a case of deja vu when a scared voice on the VHF radio called for help as he was sinking on chi bar in a 17 foot dory. I was about to report a quiet week when around 1600 on today Friday Hayling Rescue responded to the call together with the harbour patrol and Hayling Lifeboat. Bizarrely we passed a capsized 49'er on the roughest part of the bar before reaching the stricken vessel taking it in tow to stop it sinking with momentum activating the scuppers. the harbour patrol put a crew member on the dory who cleared a mooring line from around its propeller, leaving the lifeboat to deal with the 49er.after the dory regained engine power and was let go i remembered it was the same dinghy and crew that Hayling Rescue had rescued in exactly similar circumstances back in 2005. on that occasion in very rough seas hayling rescue had heaved on board the 2 elderly crew while pputting a line on the 3/4 sunk dory. the new lady crew from the harbour parol was then put on board Hayling Rescue to look over the casualties with the Hayling Lifeboat arriving to rush them ashore......cold and shaken........ having heaved the two elderly crew from Hayling Rescue into the Lifeboat the Lifeboat crew not realizing the lady was from the harbour patrol unceremoniously yanked her into the lifeboat and sped ashore. The two elderly gentlemen from Bembridge hopefully will not dice with chi bar in all its ebb tide fury again. Family fun week now just ended was a quiet affair and I think the seemingly thousands of little kids thoroughly enjoyed their adventurous week...bring on the Mengeham Regatta and HISC junior race week!

Crosby Stills Nash & Young 'Déjà vu'.

A dinghy safely towed to shore.

Hayling Rescue

August 8, 2012

Who rattled your cage then?

The two certainties of life namely death and taxation are joined by the certainty of a dinghy sailor capsizing frequently or hopefully in frequently whilst afloat. In the last 40 years or so then hayling rescue has attended one or two capsized dinghys.........Like many Sunday afternoons then Hayling Rescue was out on Chichester Bar attending capsizes on this occasion 29'ers. the fact that they had capsized in the harbour and had been swept out by a 6 knot ebb tide against afresh south westerly breeze was unfortunate. However., the boats were out training and learning so instead of hauling the kids out of the sea and back to the club it was considered that they would learn more by attempting to right their dinghies or at least drop the mainsail and get towed home.........however, there are always people watching and concerned calls came from various directions including honker...... Are you alright? Do you need help? Shall we launch the lifeboat? Eventually all the kids were brought ashore without too much drama and hopefully with valuable experience gained. .... I am reminded of the Ainsle effect after his silver medal in the laser in the 1996 Olympics. HISC hosted a laser qualifying event and had 50 extra laser radial entries from young ladies wanting to sail with their hero in Hayling Bay. The usual brisk south westerly coincided with the spring ebb tide and Hayling Rescue was entering the harbour with a rudderless radial and met a capsized Solo dinghy and crew drifting out. The Solo sailor was pulled onto Hayling Rescue and after righting the dinghy the

nubile radial sailor was put on board to steer the solo home behind a HISC rescue boat. Nearby on the Bar was an upturned Laser Radial and exhausted crew. The Laser was righted and the by now recovered solo sailor was put on board to steer home behind Hayling Rescue........The Balcony Watchers at HISC were then treated to the bewildering sight of a Solo being towed in with a nubile teenager at the helm closely followed by Hayling Rescue towing a Laser Radial with a rather senior in years Solo sailor proudly steering it. Happy Days.
Crosby Stills Nash & Young 'Déjà Vu'.

Hayling Rescue
August 13, 2012

A very quiet weekend with one bizarre incident.

The Palmer family had spotted on the winner bank an inflatable canoe with 2 ladies and 2 young kids going nowhere. Hayling Rescue went to investigate and found a Czechoslovakian family completely oblivious to wind and tide and half a mile from the beach they had launched from. They were taken on board and landed back onto their beach by the red flag..........near the spot where the Bulgarian guy lost his life earlier in the season rescuing a child swept out by the tide. Appropriate advice was given to the English speaking mother but otherwise they were oblivious to their plight. Sadly over the years Hayling Rescue has been involved in quite a few rescue dramas off this beach and so Tony's magic jukebox needs to play the plaintive 'Ebb Tide' by the Righteous Brothers and then 'Harvest of Love' by Benny Hill to cheer us up.

David Nicholls
August 13, 2012

Frank, many thanks, as Safety Leader last week it was always nice to know you were never far away. I am sure you would deny it but I did spot you pulling several wet sailors out of the oggin and a Topper towed home also. Also thanks for the 'consultancy' chats. Enjoy the break FED WEEK NEXT WEEK. Tally Ho

Hayling Rescue
August 16, 2012

The CONFESSIONAL............ Federation Week memories.........

I was reminiscing with James Yearsley on our fed week follies over the years....more in a later dispatch,but the first Hayling Rescue boat was helping in the 1984 Regatta complete with it's stenciled license...'Stena Inspectorate 22 persons' ..Timmy Hancock that famous Olympian had other ideas.In those days Dell Quay Sailing Club kindly invited competitors to their at home party on the Monday night and Timmy requested the pleasure of Hayling Rescue to take him and a few friends to said event. ..Hayling Rescue duly arrived at HISC to pick up vast hordes of Timmy's friends and over 40 people were soon packed onto the boat ....fortunatly Dick Mumford from MRSC arrived in his large dory and we off loaded some of the excess............but with all that weight we went ever so slowly that we cut our losses and drifted up the Bosham channel to spend a convivial evening instead at the anchor bleau..........It was on the way home the fun started and you will have to ask Rupert Hatfield, Barry Edgington, Fiddi or Mops Millard-Barnes of 'Sea Bear' what transpired....If they wish to confess.........More tomorrow.

Hayling Rescue

August 16, 2012

Were you or any of your friends on that jolly expedition and can we identify all 40 plus reprobates who were on that adventure. They all appear to be middle-aged pillars of the community now.

Hayling Rescue

August 17, 2012

Fed Week Confessional.........

 A tremendous amount of hard work and organisation goes into the annual Fed Week regatta.......The co-ordinator in the box 'Sandy' co-ordinates all the support and safety boats and disperses all the relevant information over the VHF radio on at least 4 different frequencies and thus requires a chatterbox mentality coupled with a grasp of the Queens English. For 4 whole days we had endured for many hours non-stop the dulcit tones of Simon Muckley who had been the Box co-ordinator for many years. After racing on the Thursday we were enjoying club dinner on the balcony and unfortunately Simon Muckley was still on a high and was pontificating loudly on some inane race management issue. This was too much for the Bishop who had had an exacting day on rescue duty. He picked up Simon's plate of chocolate profiteroles and stuffed the lot in Simon's face. In sonorous tones he exclaimed:

"I've been wanting to do that all day!"

We all laughed so much that even Simon joined in and a diplomatic incident was avoided. Talk of the balcony recalls the Johnny C incident which will be the subject of a later dispatch

Hayling Rescue

August 19, 2012

Fed Week Confessional...............

There is always a tremendous amount of hard work and devotion put in by the various committees race officers and volunteers from all around the Harbour community. Hayling Rescues therefore only plays a small though visible part in what is a tough sailing week.In terms of confessional Hayling Rescue has to hold its hands up especially if others foibles are revealed.... mistakes too many to mention.....although in terms of laying the inflatable racing marks in the wrong place there have been more protests both Official and unofficial when they have been laid in the correct place.........I must also mention in dispatches my star crew in 2000 Ian 'Puffer' Williams who on 14 separate occasions took on the Jacques Cousteau role on a very windy monday.....It only remains for me to wish all the competitors and organisers a sparkling racing week...... but I hope you enjoy the post activities even more......Now Tony's magic juke box needs to play 'The Carnival is Over' by The Seekers.........nothing sinister intended.

The Seekers - 'The Carnival Is Over'

Out on the Harbour Bar. HR is a welcome sight when your Flying Fifteen is full of water.

The crew climb to safety aboard HR

HR stands off while the FF skipper sorts out a towing line

HR tows the sunken Flying Fifteen back to shore.

Hayling Rescue

August 23, 2012

Fed Week Confessional.........

Like Christmas dinner there is a lot of preparation, it is a long time coming and is over in a flash..... but tonight is the fabled HISC Fed Week party......I have often likened it to the opening sequences to the film Zulu......... however shenanigans at previous Fed Week Thursdays or the reporting thereof have necessarily been censored. It only remains therefore for me to wish you a Merry Christmas if and when it comes.

Hayling Rescue

August 26, 2012

Never deny the working man his day of leisure...........

Fed week came and went and coffee with the Bishop on the balcony on Saturday morning was followed by a relatively quiet afternoon as only windsurfers were out enjoying the strong breeze......However a call came through to nip out into Hayling Bay and tow back a motor boat with engine failure to Mill Rythe.......... in the prevailing conditions there were no other boats out in the bay apart from a 17 foot leisure angling boat lying to anchor in a rough heavy swell. The engine had stopped..........The vessel was duly taken in tow enjoying wild surfing conditions on Chi Bar.....and then it started to rain......We got back to Mill Rythe without further mishap ....I must not be so judgmental after all it is August bank holiday weekend and the working man must be allowed to enjoy his day of leisure angling......Over to you Tony...

'Gone Fishin' - Louis Armstrong & Bing Crosby.

Hayling Rescue

August 26, 2012

Sunday Sunday can't trust that day......

Sunday started too quietly.... The Bishop had gone to Winchester so there was no morning coffee on the balcony ..then a club member rang and reported his RIB. broken free from its mooring and on the high tide line on Thorney Island beach and would I kindly go and get it on the next high tide ...7.30 p. m.....so that was Evensong cancelled...then the Coastguard wanted a broken down Jet Ski sorted out off the beach near the novelty rock emporium and this was taken in tow to the HISC slipway the Sea Start wanted a broken down motor cruiser with small children on board sorted out off East Head and this was towed to Sparkes to be refueled.....as was Hayling Rescue...then the HISC office re[ported an RS800 with a broken mast on the Pilsey Sands and this was towed back to the club and then Hayling Rescue proceed to Thorney Island beach to recover the errant RIB which was towed back to its mooring then Hayling Rescue was tidied up and hosed down then it was time to dash to the Farm Stores for something to eat and drink overnight on My Lord's Pond mooring....... a large Galaxy chocolate bar washed down with a carton of Cranberry Juice......sort that one out Tony...

The Cranberries - 'Just My Imagination'.

Hayling Rescue

August 27, 2012

Postscript.......

We had nearly reached My Lords Pond sanctuary on Sunday with a chocolate supper beckoning when the mobile phone rang.....

"Roger from the Harbour office here we have just had a resident of West Wittering ring to report a kite surfer in difficulties near Pilsey Island as we have locked up the patrol boat for the night we wondered if you would nip over and sort it out"......

"But ..but... oh alright then...."

The kite surfer was duly located but his friend in a Rib had turned up to give him a lift home. Hayling Rescue then retired to sanctuary pleases that he had bought an extra choc bar....Cadburys Wispa for the delayed feast....... 'Oh Happy Day' on the magic juke box please Tony.....

Edwin Hawkins Singers - 'Oh Happy Day'.

John Rees
August 27, 2012

Tuesday of fed week, loud crack, tacked on it, after much searching found a shroud plate had gone, trying to think of a get out of jail plan, no shroud on one tack and heading due south, and there he is - right place right time, the only boat I trust to get me home, yet again I owe you Hayling Rescue, will save until the dark days of winter and make sure it is more than a Cadbury's Wispa.

Hayling Rescue
August 30, 2012

I knew at the age of 8 I would never make a mechanic. My Xmas present of a Meccano set taught me never to go near a spanner, let alone a nut and bolt. Thus it was with much fear and trepidation that I decided after a cup of coffee with the Bishop on the club balcony that I must fit the new hydraulic pump which had arrived for Hayling Rescue's water jet unit, the old one nearly dead and often malfunctioning. Fortunately the financial friends of Hayling Rescue had saved the day yet again with the 500 odd quid needed for the purchase. The old pump would probably fail before Basher Bashall could fit the new one on the weekend. So it was that I bit the bullet to do the ten minute job with 4 nuts and bolts and a hydraulic pipe to switch over. An hour and a half later and after much cursing and swearing (I often call myself a blithering idiot) the job was done and after a test run the 2nd windsurfer of the week who had hit the Winner Bank and broken his skeg was duly rescued drifting out of the harbour. Tony's magic juke box should find a song for the cackhanded mechanic

Elvis Costello & The Attractions - 'Pump it Up' 1978

Lana and Andy Kelsey get a lift to their Wedding Reception.

Hayling Rescue

September 9, 2012

It never ceases to amaze me at what happens at sea..........

After a relatively quiet spell Sunday looked as if things could be in the offing.....Having said cheerio to David Nichols on the club pontoon, Hayling Rescue nipped out to chi bar with the intention of seeing the RS Nationals event competitors safely home. However a RIB from another sailing club dug its bow into a wave and the inflatable collar separated from the hull nearly as far as the transom leaving the crew treading water...............They sent out a distress call to the coastguard and Hayling Rescue appeared...as if by magic....within several seconds.....the crew had not noticed Hayling Rescue lurking nearby. The crew were taken off and the various bits were towed to HISC..Iwas reminded that I nearly suffered the same fate earlier in the year when Hayling Rescue crashed into a big wave whilst rushing to the aid of a capsized 29'er. Fortunately only the bow fendering was ripped off and evensong was again canceled whilst my large can of impact adhesive was put to good use...............Having had a peep at XC weather for the coming week I note there are some breezy days for the windsurfers.............

Hayling Rescue

September 28, 2012

September is always a quiet month and as Dave Hollies is missing the usual epistles I thought I would sprout forth with another missive....Having missed Dave's company for coffee on the balcony the last week or so has seen much rain...................hayling rescue has attended a number of minor incidents...a kayaker, a windsurfer, a yacht with an engine failure and a yacht broken adrift from the club moorings during last Monday's gale. Jacques Cousteau came into his element diving under a yacht to find out why there was not much happening when the engine was used. A big growth of weed on the propeller was the problem and the old scrubbing brush was utilized. Moving boats from moorings to boatyards for winter lay up is this seasons main activity and in the last couple of days Hayling Rescue has towed a large trimaran from the Nutbourne Channel to My Lord's Pond and a yacht from the Itchenor moorings to Thornham Marina.....whilst this commercial work does not bring in many pennies it does help buy the blocks of cheese and chocolate which Hayling Rescue lives on...It is therefore fortunate that I usually get treated to coffee on the balcony by the Bishop, Dave Hollies or Brian C.B.

Dr. Feelgood - 'Milk And Alcohol'

Hayling Rescue

October 5, 2012

THE SLOOP JOHN B....

there is always something going on in chi har...so on a quiet sunday afternoon when the voodoo phone came to life it was either gong to be a double glazing salesman or someone needing assistance.........

"Good afternoon is that Hayling Rescue.....I wonder if you can help....We have had a row with the skipper and want to jump ship....but he won't land us ashore and we can't last another night on board....we want to be taken off ......"

Hayling Rescue sped to the scene wondering if he would need a muscat or cutlass and whether he would need to swing through the rigging to effect a rescue upon arrival 2 brothers were ready on the foredeck and jumped ship complete with baggage......being wary of fisticuffs, Hayling Rescue inquired where the skipper was....

"When we told him you were coming he went below decks and locked himself in........"

Hayling Rescue took the two crew back to Chi Marina and their car.........

"Thank you very much for your help we just could not spend another minute on board....we had a frightful row with the captain........ and our father can be quite a hard man when he wants to be...... "

Hayling Rescue returned to HISC just in time to rescue a windsurfer drifting out to see on the fast flowing ebb tide......I think we all know what record Tony's magic juke box will play

Lonnie Donegan 'I Wanna Go Home' Wreck of the Sloop John B.

Hayling Rescue

October 15, 2012

There is always something going on in Chi Harbour and it is always very difficult to gear up what exactly hayling rescue should be doing.Having spent Saturday and Sunday checking on the various fleets racing in the area (RS 200 EVENT, Moth Open, Harbour challenge etc.) Hayling Rescue found no incidents.......however a broken down motor boat was towed back to Northney Marina from Emsworth and a leisure angling boat was towed into Sparkes from the Nab Tower area with a fishing net around its propeller which Jacques Cousteau dived on the following morning with a sharp knife I was reflecting on the lack of overnight action with regard to the absence of a professional fishing fleet..........however 5.30 on Monday morning a professional fisherman called on the voodoophone to report an engine failure and was very cold having been adrift for 4 hours he and his boat which had a brand new engine were towed back to Northney Marina..........over any 24 hour period it is impossible to predict what might happen rescue wise..........maybe Tony's magic juke box can come up with a suitable response.

Hayling Rescue

October 21, 2012

Christmas Day (and night) with the seals.......

Sunday morning was fairly quiet so Hayling Rescue made his annual visit to see the seals and 11 of them were hauled out on the first bank. Back in 1993 there had only been 3 seals in that particular colony and Hayling rescue had his Christmas dinner with them on a crisp Dec. 25th. Red Leicester cheese on granary bread washed down with a half bottle of champagne was the Xmas fayre and jolly good it was too.Three years ago on Christmas night a lone seal came up Mengeham Creek and climbed on board the transom platform of Hayling Rescue whilst I was listening to a concert on Classic FM wrapped up in the usual 2 sleeping bags. He must have enjoyed the visit so much he returned the following night and had a two hour kip on said platform. The following night i left out a whole Christmas pudding to show I was a good host but he never reappeared. Over the years Hayling Rescue has done quite a few scatterings of ashes and last year a good friend whose wife had just died requested a special scattering...... So up we went for the deceased and family to visit the seals and then we retired to a quiet location where we held the final service ..We read out humorous poems the deceased had written just before she died and then scattered her ashes over the back of Hayling Rescue at which juncture a seal appeared and watched the proceedings giving it due reverence.... I might just return the visit this coming Christmas day ....if I can find a shop on Sandy Point that sells Red Leicester cheese........A very merry Christmas to you all...if and when it comes.

Hayling Rescue

October 30, 2012

Oysters Oysters.......

Having just got back from towing a yacht from Emsworth Harbour to Thornham Marina Hayling Rescue was greeted on the balcony with a hot cup of coffee from the Bishop (where was Dave Nichols?) and we then watched various commercial fishing boats enter the Harbour ready for the start of the Oyster trawling season on Nov. 1st. Over the years Hayling Rescue has towed a number of these vessels back to base after engine failures and Jacques Cousteau has had to dive underneath to clear the propellers of nets and rope on at least 6 occassions........very bracing on a cold January morning. A few years ago one vessel sank on its way back to Emsworth Quay in a gale and the young crew managed to swim ashore on Thorney. I thought back to the last time I had a dozen oysters and I can dispel the myth that they are an aphrodisiac, as only 4 worked..........over to you Tony.....

Elkie Brooks - 'Pearl's a Singer' 1977

Hayling Rescue

October 31, 2012

Double century ...again....

October has been relatively quiet rescue wise.....However noel Coward who was not a windsurfer, once said to Ian Fleming

"Getting drunk is rather like adultery.... you can see it coming , you can't avoid it and it leaves you with a frightful headache."

So it was rather inevitable that with 35 knots of wind a windsurfer or 2 would need rescuing.....these incidents brought the total for the year to 201 rescue incidents dealt with by Hayling Rescue with 2 months still to go. Hayling Rescue does keep a log both for official purposes and for analyzing trends and lessons learned.....There have been a number of occasions this year when Hayling Rescue has found himself on chi bar in a raging ebb tide with a capsized dinghy which capsized in the harbour......a prompt righting on first capsizing is to be encouraged........no faffing around over to Tony and his magic jukebox for musical accompaniment.

Hayling Rescue

November 29, 2012

Hayling Rescue was sitting in the sunshine on the balcony with the bishop and a cup of coffee but no Dave Nichols and remarking on the kind people who wished Hayling Rescue a happy birthday....How many more years to do thought I? Probably Hayling Rescue will go on till 2021 but 2026 is the target particularly as my self-employed persons pension plan will click in on that day......also when I cannot climb back into Hayling Rescue from the water unaided or pull a casualty out of the water unaided then I might go early...however my doctor says I am a boring patient as each time I go for the usual 5 year medicals the results of the tests are the same as the previous ones.....In the meantime I have long thought of plans to write adventure stories on my beloved South Downs......the many spooky towers....the hidden ancient churches (Have you ever been to Up Marden?)...the mystical woods and forests and places such as Kingly Vale, the Trundle, Chanctonbury Ring, Stanstead Forest, and of course the delightful pubs in hidden valleys.........so many secrets to reveal......well never mind, back to sea rescue for the next few years.

Hayling Rescue on patrol.

Hayling Rescue

December 1, 2012

I just knew it would happen.......

Hayling Rescue does not usually do commercial work at weekends so as to cover club activities and other Harbour users needing rescue in the Chi Harbour entrance so when coffee in the canteen was interrupted by a club member in his yacht with an engine failure up at Dell Quay and needing to make Emsworth marina on the tide it was an angry Hayling Rescue which made the long journey up to Fishbourne.....nothing much happened on the long tow but just as Emsworth was reached a yacht was reported sinking in Chi harbour entrance. Hayling Lifeboat was obviously launched but when their portable pump was deployed it failed to stop the ingress of water and with no lift out facilities immediately available Hayling Rescue was requested with its fabled electric portable bilge pumps, 5 are carried in the ark of the covenant. Hayling Rescue therefore left Emsworth Marina in some haste (sorry) and sped back down the harbour to help. Like those fabled recent dozen oysters of which only 3 worked

Hayling Rescue found that only 2 of his bilge pumps worked.....but this was enough to keep the yacht afloat until a crane crew arrived at Sparkes Marina to crane the yacht ashore......... Sadly I think that Hayling Rescue will refuse to do any commercial work at weekends in order to be around for the inevitable............. A Happy Advent to one and all.

Hayling Rescue

December 2, 2012

Fortunately with some of the club pontoon removed Hayling Rescue has had to swim out to his boat at half tide and above with fins and surf board ...and for coming ashore.........thus it was with no trepidation that Hayling Rescue responded to a call for Jacques Cousteau to dive underneath an angling boat which had been towed into Sparkes Marina by the Hayling Lifeboat after becoming disabled out to sea with a lobster pot marker buoy jammed around its propeller. fortunately the air temperature was just above freezing whilst the sea temperature was a balmy 8 degrees centigrade. Jacques therefore had no hesitation diving underneath the boat with mask and snorkel fins wet suit and dry suit and neoprene diving hood. This combination together with a bread knife especially sharpened by John in the HISC kitchen resulted in the rope and marker buoy being released from around the propeller and the angling boat returned seawards to its days sport. Hayling Rescue can recommend winter swimming as way back in 19.. he went surfing at weekends at Eastoke Point. That winter was colds and flue free...........Here's hoping your Advent Season is free from the sniffles........Oh, I forgot to mention that the dive also cured a migraine headache that was building after a supper of a huge bar of chocolate and 4 mince pies courtesy of the Bishop and Brian CB

Hayling Rescue

December 2, 2012

2012. Rescue Incident 211....oh dear....

It is always a mistake to take off wetsuit and dry suit too early on a Sunday. Having been so attired since the diving incident some 4 hours previously Jacques was made aware from a number of sources that a 43 foot yacht had run aground on the Winner Bank on a raging ebb tide ......having just changed into civvies Jacques was not best pleased . A leap into the dry suit was followed by a quick swim out to Hayling Rescue on the island hammerhead and a rendezvous with the Hayling lifeboat alongside the stricken yacht resulted in the Hayling lifeboat towing the yacht ahead with Hayling Rescue leaning the yacht on its side from a masthead halyard so as to reduce it's draught...After a bit of power from both boats the yacht was eventually pulled off the notorious shingle bank into the main channel...Hayling Rescue returned to the hammerhead and Jacques swam ashore with fins and the surf board. Changing once again out of the dry suit, Jacques noticed damage to a velcro seal........so the glue will make a comeback tomorrow. I prefer a wetsuit because you always know you are going to get wet........with a drysuit you can stay dry until....................... then you have major problems. If only someone could design a wetsuit which is quick to put on for emergencies and keeps the wearer warm when its windy things would be a lot safer

Tony Aitken

December 3, 2012 · London

So sad the news about Dee Mackonochie, as a hugely well respected balcony grumblie, she is greatly missed with her unforgiving fearless humour, she might even forgive the split infinitives...

Hayling Rescue

December 9, 2012

Were not all Rob Roys you know....

There was Dasher and Dancer, Prancer and Vixen, not to mention Comet, Cupid, Donner and Blitzen and Peter, and this year joined by BASHER Bashall who had kindly done a few repairs to Hayling Rescue just before Hayling Rescue made the long journey from Sparkes to HISC carrying Father Christmas to the children's Christmas party. Father Christmas duly alighted on the HISC pontoon to be greeted by numerous kids. One six year old told Father Christmas ......

"I know who you are...." Oh calamity thinks H R.....

"You are Colin Ralph..."

"No ....I am not." The kid is informed,

"I am Father Christmas and F C does not speak in a broad Scottish accent." Says I, in my cultured Portsmouth dialect

"And no I did not go to PGS........."

"But, but, but..." Says the disillusioned six year old....

"Colin is always dressed up in silly costumes......"

"I can assure you laddie Father Christmas does not wear a kilt......."

Honour was restored and Hayling Re.....er sorry, Father Christmas joined the little revelers in the clubhouse handing out presents before melting away into the night..........may I take this opportunity to wish all my readers a Merry Christmas and a brave happy good new year. Peace be unto you........Merry Christmas.

Father Christmas.

Hayling Rescue

December 19, 2012

For those of you interested in the latest on the ketch motor sailor sunk on the Emsworth moorings, Hayling Rescue duly went up to investigate 6.15 a.m. yesterday. The vessel is completely sunk in 10 feet of water at low water springs...so a little bit complicated for Jacques Cousteau/Hayling Rescue........it will need a salvage barge and a team of four divers to sort out. I will keep you updated.

What does Hayling Rescue do at Christmas....part two of a grand epic...........It was late on Christmas Eve when Hayling Rescue arrived back with the tug aground on the Pilsey Sands. The mysterious crew looked even more sinister in the darkness. The tug needed 6 foot to float and the depth coming up yo high tide was............5 feet 9 inches... A sturdy rope was passed and for the next hour the two boats banged and crashed their way across the sand until the Emsworth Channel was reached and the tug was free of the ground. It was escorted into Sparkes Marina where the owner Nick R viewed with some dismay his military looking visitors......I don't think he challenged them for berthing fees! Hayling Rescue then found a nice sheltered spot in the Marina to listen to a repeat of the service of carols on the BBC World Service at 0100......... unfortunately......... this

33

coincided with closing time at a party in the Mariners Bar on the Marina...when a full scale punch up spilled out into the night with much shouting swearing and screaming. The Kings College Choir had just started 'Silent Night' but fight the good fight would have been apt. HR therefore missed his beloved carols for the second time..............Christmas Day morning arrived, the Israelis left for the Bay of Biscay and Hayling Rescue journeyed to East Head,found a quiet sand dune and listened to a second repeat of said Carol service on Radio 3..............without interruption.........

Coming next another Christmas drama ...."I am a Yachtsman you know." A rescue drama from Christmas 1994.

Hayling Rescue

December 21, 2012

Hayling Rescue at Christmas..... the second story in an occasional series.....

Todays epic is entitled "I am a yachtsman you know"........

It was Boxing Day1994 and muggins had nipped round to the Driscolls for an evening feast of gammon bubble and squeak and jacket potato with loads of butter....when the RNLI lifeboat pager went off..i did both in those days...The Lifeboat duly launched into a gale force 8 sou'wester to a motor cruiser aground on the stocker sands. The 18 crew and one dog had had an epic day.. chi marina to the folly inn...lunch and back to chi all well and good with a completely sober skipper and first mate but like we all do had clipped the edge of east head near Dunes and stuck fast with a couple of hours of a spring ebb to go. We went alongside and it was obvious the more merry of those on board would have to come off so we evacuated 16 people and one dog. Although all went smoothly in the wild conditions one evacuee who had made best use of the facilities at the folly kept shouting out to whoever would listen....

"I am a yachtsman you know"......

We left the scene and took the whole circus back to Itchenor Jetty and landed them safely in the heavy rain and wind which had increased to a force nine.. However a lone voice still pierced the deepening gloom.....

"I am a yachtsman you know....I am a yachtsman you know..."

At this the patience of one of my crew snapped and he bellowed back

"If you were a bloody yachtsman you would not have put your bloody yacht aground"

Silence reigned in the rain and we took the lifeboat back into the teeth of the gale to Sparkes Marina prior to helping those left on the motor cruiser at East Head.....this epic adventure is to be told in Part 2 of "I am a yachtsman you know."

Hayling Rescue

December 21, 2012

Hayling Rescue at Christmas....."I am a yachtsman you know." Part 2......

It was boxing day night and back at Sparkes we were listening to the latest shipping forcast...Wight...severe gale force 9 increasing storm force 10....rain ..good....It was therefore decided that muggins would transfer to his own boat Hayling Rescue and the RNLI lifeboat would act as escort if things went wrong. At midnight the 2 boats left Sparkes Marina and having arrived at East Head found zero visibility in the storm. We feared the worst...up on the shore on east head spit.Where were the crew? Eventually out of the darkness the motor cruiser appeared unlit due to an electrical failure and it motored clear of the beach. We escorted the boat up to the Itchenor Jetty and after a half hour battle we managed to pull the vessel alongside to secure........Hayling Lifeboat and Hayling Rescue then bounced down the Harbour in complete darkness and heavy rain eventually finding the entrance to Sparkes Marina and then securing the 2 boats alongside a bucking pontoon.....all went quiet save for the shriek of the gale in the rigging of the many yachts parked up.....when an eerie voice screamed out.......

"I am a yachtsman you know...."

Hayling Rescue

December 21, 2012

Thursday update on sunken Ketch Emsworth moorings....Hayling Rescue went up to the scene with professional diving team, Richard Blake from Hayling Yacht Co. and rendezvoud with the Harbour patrol. The divers made a thorough survey and it is a big job which we will all undertake on Jan. 2nd and 3rd. The boats name is 'Boomerang' and I suppose it prefers life 'Down under.'

Hayling Rescue

December 24, 2012

Hayling Rescue at Christmas.....the last in a series of epic yuletide adventures.........

It was Christmas Day a few years ago....sunny and dry...(what?).....and HR. had just finished an early morning walk on East Head. 2 Yachts from Sparkes Marina sailed by and beckoned me to join them. I tied up behind the larger of the two and we sailed in tandem picking up a quiet mooring opposite Itchenor Sailing Club. The yacht's skipper was quite decadent as he not only had a microwave on board but also a sound system to rival the Stones.... so we had piping hot vol au vents accompanied by the 1812 overture at full blast. We then went are separate ways with the 2nd yacht taking the first yachts skippers wife back to Sparkes to prepare Christmas dinner for twenty guests at their nearby house while he carried on enjoying his sail around the harbour......

"Don't be late back she warned him........"

Later that afternoon HR was returning from a long walk along Hayling seafront eying the impending sunset over the Isle of Wight when a lady walking her dog

35

came up and said.......

"What time is high tide?".......

"It was 3 hours ago." Says HR.........

"Oh dear..." Said the lady.

"That yachtsman will miss his Christmas dinner........."

"What yachtsman where....?"

"Hard aground on that tide gauge opposite the club..." She replied......

I legged it back to the club at some great pace and jumped aboard Hayling Rescue and motored across to the yacht which was lying half on its side . The skipper had already made ready the main halyard from the masthead and HR made fast and leaned the yacht over on its side and then pulled it off the tide gauge spit into deep water. HR.then went alongside to return the halyard and the skipper gave profuse thanks and said....

"As you know my wife would kill me if I missed our Christmas dinner...."

Not she or the twenty guests ever heard of the little drama........I hope you all have a brave New Year

Hayling Rescue

December 27, 2012

Thursday 27 Dec. Rescue incident 215 for year 2012.

11am. 30 knots of breeze.......A man attempted to row out to his fishing boat sinking on its mooring off Itchenor Jetty. His dinghy overturned and he was left clinging to the mooring buoy . Hayling Lifeboat and Hayling Rescue responded to the emergency call although Hayling Rescue was a little slow getting underway having to swim out to his boat on the hammerhead being high tide. After a high speed dash both boats arrived on scene to find that a passing yacht called 'Dragonfly' had picked the man out of the water and landed him on Itchenor Jetty and he was okay. Hayling Rescue then deployed one of his pumps on the sinking fishing boat until it was safe and both boats returned to Hayling Island. ....an incident of this sort always happens at Christmas particular as in the seemingly endless wild weather people are unable to care properly for their boats afloat on moorings.

Hayling Rescue

December 27, 2012

Hayling Rescue was compiling the rescue statistics for the year when interrupted for the 215 incident but on return the figures were brought up to date............Was 2012 really that busy? Apart from normal escort duty during club racing and the usual commercial work....Towing boats from moorings to boatyard for winter lay up and vice versa....actual rescue incidents attended included the righting of 39 capsized dinghys...13 vessels with broken masts towed to safety......50 vessels towed to safety with engine failures 18 yachts aground attended and pulled into deep water....12 dives under boats to clear fouled propellors.....19 windsurfers brought ashore in various states of repair!!!!.....9 sinking vessels attended and a variety of other incidents...fortunately only 6 incidents were overnight.......roll on 2013.

HR providing safety cover for swimmers during preparations for the Charity fund raising 'Swim for Simone' at HISC.

Hayling Rescue

December 31, 2012

KISS OF DEATH........

HR. was having coffee but not on the balcony with the bishop and other club worthies during new years eve morning. Simon Payne had kindly come up to wish everyone a happy new year and remarked to HR. that it had been quiet on the FB front with no recent HR. postings to laugh at....This comment could only be the kiss of death. The rain was beating down on the club windows with the 30 knot breeze occasionally gusting to 35.......when 2 windsurfers knocked on the door.

"....er ...er... Charlie Hawtrey has not been seen for half an hour, he was last seen near that pole leading up up to MRSC. having fallen in."

So HR donned wetsuit, swam out to boat on hammerhead and with the 2 windsurfers as crew sped to the scene......notthing found....oh dear thinks H.R. ......I will shortly have to inform the Coastguard who will probably launch the Hayling Lifeboat and scramble the rescue helicopter!!! A search along the

Tournerbury shore was in process when out of the mist appeared said windsurfer...all okay having had to make repairs to his rig on the beach..........Is this to be the last rescue incident of 2012?.....HR will keep his wetsuit on for the rest of the day.........If only to act as insurance against another incident........It is pertinent at this juncture to pay my deep gratitude to Simon and Mr. Zhik for supplying said wetsuit.... a very warm and well designed combination and probably the best I have had over the last 42 years...... the first being a rather fancy water skier's wetsuit with the painful gusset and poppers to keep the jacket in place.................. A BRAVE NEW YEAR TO YOU ALL.

Hayling Rescue

January 2, 2013

Like the Windmill Theatre......we never close

2013 opened with Hayling Rescue pumping out a yacht low in the water on the Bosham moorings and then recovering a big mooring buoy drifting down the harbour and then on scene to cover the MRSC race winkle of the harbour with about 25 boats competing and no mishaps.On Jan 2nd HR had just finished coffee with the Bishop when the voodoophone summoned him to a motor boat with an engine failure off Mill Rythe needing a tow back to Northney Marina. Tomorrow....Jan 3rd Golden Arrow Marine come down to give a major service to the engine of HR........and to trace a small leak of hydraulic oil from the gearbox.......If serious we might have to put the shutters up and change our logo to we sometimes close.......

Hayling Rescue

January 4, 2013

We never close continued....

Golden Arrow Marine duly came down to do a major service on the engine of Hayling Rescue and all is well save for a couple of oil seals to be replaced on the gearbox.....In the 1980s and the 1990s the first Hayling Rescue used to be lifted out at Sparkes boatyard for its winter refit after the last HISC race at the end of each year to be relaunched just before the first race of the new year in march....but my how times change........in the mid 1990s HR had been lifted and stripped down for its refit when it had to be relaunched in less than a day in support of a major salvage operation for an errant yacht on the Chidham beach. The following year HR was not going to be caught out and most of the refit was being done alongside at Sparkes, so yours truly, one mild January day was busy applying a nice bright orange neoprene coat of paint to the bow of HR when the coastguard had a report of a frigate ashore at west wittering..........An annoyed HR proceeded at once wondering whether it was the start of the Russian invasion or a Royal Navy navigator was having a bad hair day.. HR arrived on scene to find HMS Dittisham rolling in the surf off west wittering beach........it was an old HMS Dittisham a former minesweeper used as a sea cadets HQ in Dartmouth but now on its way to the Thames for a refit. The new owner had lost his crew to injury the day before and having had one engine blow up he sought refuge in dear old chi harbour without a chart. A towline was passed and as it was just coming up to high tide we were able to coax the vessel over the Winner Bank to the main channel. The skipper followed HR into the working pontoon area of Sparkes boatyard where the entire workforce was needed to heave the vessel safely alongside (A minesweeper is not easy to steer on one engine) HR helped by nudging the bow and stern and amidships with the newly painted bow of HR leaving 3 very loud orange marks on HMS Dittisham........ The skipper completed repairs and left a fortnight later for the Thames but the vessel was eventually scrapped at Pounds yard in portsmouth.....Now you have a good idea why HR is always on stand by proudly (I HOPE!) like the Windmill Theatre... WE NEVER CLOSE...

Hayling Rescue

February 2, 2013

That is what friends are for............

With there being no rescue dramas to report for January I thought another rescue drama from the past might act as a stopgap......So it was sometime in the 1990's when I was also a crew member of the RNLI Hayling Lifeboat. I was at the station helping polish up the Lifeboat for its quarterly inspection by Head Officer, when Natalie, who was the book keeper at HISC rang through to report a dead body drifting past the club. So not wanting to ruin our preparations for the grand inspection, muggins duly went out in Hayling Rescue to retrieve the poor unfortunate. The body was located on the Pilsey Sands and heaved on board.........A naked 5ft 8in 36-24-36, blonde beauty..... A lifelike inflatable doll with a gift tag tied to the left nipple which read.....

"To Chief Petty Officer Jones, enjoy your 6 month deployment on HMS Warship."

Hayling Rescue landed the betrothed into the care of the crane crew at Sparkes boatyard and the police were stood down.....However one of my Lifeboat friends had phoned the Sport newspaper with the scoop, and a photographer and reporter were on their way. Fortunately the crane crew, unimpressed with the dolls statistics had joined up the inflation valve to the boatyard compressor.........an explosion ensued and the doll was blown to pieces thwarting the photographer of a humiliating scoop.

The next morning I crept into the newsagents and purchased The Sport much to the disgust of the assistant.....The story....without photo ...had made page 3 and Hayling Rescue had its day of fame.......fortunately very few Islanders buy the Sport so the drama went largely unnoticed although my friend got his revenge for one of my earlier practical jokes.

Hayling Rescue

March 10, 2013

There is always something going on in Chi Har........

Saturday evening saw the ace Fundraising Friends of Hayling Rescue strut their stuff at HISC with the Bishop, Dave Hollies, and the ace auctioneer excelling themselves and a full report and credits is to follow. The ace fun raiser, Billy Boy Masterman also excelled bidding for and winning a days sailing tuition kindly donated by ace coach Melvyn Cooper.......he also delayed HR's return to his boat by keeping him in the bar until gone midnight ....However having wrapped himself snugly in 2 sleeping bags HR was woken up within minutes by the night watchman at Sparkes reporting a yacht aground in the marina entrance and so muggins went to sea and found a 38 foot yacht aground on the tide gauge spit opposite HISC. It was too late to refloat the yacht on the ebbing tide and Muggins returned to the marina eventually getting to sleep at 3 of the clock.....only to get up at 5 to return to the stricken yacht.........However the heavy yacht had dug a hole for itself in the sand and HR eventually pulled the yacht which had an engine failure to the safety of the marina at 7.30.......which meant muggins found himself at the front of the breakfast queue at HISC by 08.00........ A full report on the fundraising evening is imminent.......QED.

David Nicholls

March 11, 2013 · Hayling

The Friends of Hayling Rescue wish to thank the immense generosity of those who provided items for the Tombola, Balloon Lottery, and Auctions. They also wish to thank those who bought tickets, bid on items and donated to the handsome sum that now exceeds £8250.00.

An extremely enjoyable evening was had by all, with 144 guests attending, and other placing proxy bids from as far a field as California.

In true HR fashion, following the dinner and during the small hours our hero went to the aid of a stricken yacht that was aground in the harbour. The good work continues everyday, very much thanks to your philanthropy.

Many Thanks.

Friends of Hayling Rescue.

Hayling Rescue

April 2, 2013

MY DAY OFF....

My pal on the Chi Har patrol berated me last year for not having at least one day off a week from the rescue scene and I attempted to have Tuesdays off, but my customers thought otherwise. And so Today Tuesday I attempted to have MY DAY OFF to stop me becoming stale and tired........It was not to be as the voodoophone clattered into life at nine with a lady in tears as her boat had sunk on its mooring in Fishery Creek......the harbour patrol having been unable to salvage it on Easter Monday so on MY DAY OFF I took Hayling Rescue up said creek and with much difficulty eventually towed the errant motor cruiser into Sparkes Marina where the crane driver expertly lifted the boat upside down out of the water spinning the vessel the right way up which revealed the name of the boat painted proudly on the bow.................'MY DAY OFF'!

Hayling Rescue

April 3, 2013

As there has been little to report rescue wise recently I thought another epic adventure from the past would fill the gap..........

Big Bernie and John the Fish were 2 lobster fishermen who operated a large dirty catamaran lobster fishing boat out of Sparkes........you would not want to bump into them on a bright day let alone on a dark night ....and they did not take prisoners....Their idea of a fun day was to go out at 0400 in the morning tending their 650 lobster pots in Sandown Bay returning late afternoon with the catch.....7 days a week.....and so one day in the early 2000s I was working on HR in Sparkes when the voodoophone came to life...

"Good afternoon......."

"Get out here f.....g fast it's John we have hit an underwater obstruction ripped out one of our prop shafts and we are f...... sinking......"

"Where are you...?"

"Out at the f...... Nab Tower......"

Hayling Rescue has a reasonable turn of speed so it did not take long to cover the ten miles or so...chuck my 2 electronic portable bilge pumps on board the lobster boat, catch John's tow line and tie it on my towing bollard. We steamed full speed to Sparkes intending to beach the sinking vessel on a mud berth which would dry out in an hour and we had an hour and a bit at full belt etc.. .John the fish disappeared below decks with the pumps and I set course for Chi Har....Only for a Royal Navy Destroyer to appear undoubtedly on a collision course....would the insurance policy cover this calamity and would I lose the no claims bonus?.... We both held our collision course only for me to chicken out and change my course to pass astern of the destroyer......At this violent maneuver John's head appeared from out of the bilges .....

"What the f... is going on?"

"Royal Navy..." I shout.....

"F... the Navy, Chi Har is that way!" Shouts John.........at which I altered course for a Naval contretemps only for the destroyer to think better and it turned away to Bracklesham Bay…

We made it back to Sparkes mud berth with seconds to spare and John the fish was soon sooner over the side fitting a spare prop shaft through the hole so he could go fishing on the 4 o'clock tide the next morning......f.....g hell…

Hayling Rescue

April 21, 2013

Strange things happen at sea.....

So there we were having an HISC breakfast before matins with Basher Bashall, the Bishop and Chris Driscoll, who is making a steady recovery from a knee operation. Chris was talking about the kindness shown by a Chi Har sailing celeb.....Bev Moss would probably have given him rock star status, who had paid him a visit during his convalescence and spent a couple of hours talking about old times. Of course I am always castigated by the Bishop when I say that everything in this world is connected.....

"Another one of your silly conspiracy theories." He chants.........

So anyway 4 hours later Voodoophone comes to life, and a local boatyard is asking me to tow home a customer who has an engine failure on his RIB off of Seaview IOW. Muggins therefore proceeds out to said location only to find that the distressed mariner is...................The sailing celeb talked about at Breakfast......stick that one in your mitre, Bishop!............

Anyway the celeb and his boat were duly towed home to Chi Har........incidentally, having mentioned Bev Moss, NEVER ask him to tell you the story of Prince Charming, the melon and Cinderella.........or Hammersmith Broadway..............it only remains for me to wish you all a joyful summer if and when it comes

Hayling Rescue

April 22, 2013

Jacques Cousteau lives..........

But I bet he did not get by on just 2 cups of coffee during a busy day...........Thus it was that I woke up Monday morning with one hell of a dehydration headache...Only for voodoophone coming to life with a yachtsman with a brand new folding propeller suspecting it it had pinged off on his first manoeuvre astern and could I dive underneath PRONTO to check before he splashed out 450 quid plus 2 way crainage fees. With a thumping head and Zhik wetsuit under a drysuit Jacques Cousteau duly dived underneath to find the propellor.....................gone!..........Jacques returned to HISC for coffee with the Bishop and C-B with the avowed intention of 2 cartons of orange juice to accompany those balcony coffees daily.

John Rees

April 28, 2013

Thanks for your help today Frank, was about to 'borrow' a club rib that someone had left on the pontoon with the keys in, sure you handled the situation, if there was on, better than I.

Hayling Rescue

April 28, 2013

That sinking feeling.......

The weekend proved to be just as busy as it threatened........that 14.30 squall on Saturday afternoon resulted in 5 casualties attended by Hayling Rescue as well as a 40 foot yacht running aground on west mud....north of the starboard hand mark...all incidents were within half a mile of hisc which is very often the case....Sunday morning saw Sparkes Marina have a drama with their fuel jetty so Hayling Rescue had to go up to Northney Marina to refuel which cost all of muggins' cash.....but then SeaStart, the AA of the sea, had a customer up the Fowley Rythe reporting his yacht, launched on Friday, sinking on its mooring............HR arrived therefore in less than 5 minutes and with 2 portable pumps soon had the vessel seaworthy enough to tow into Emsworth Marina....The tooth abcess....the size of a golf ball even behaved and with Mike

O'Connor's patent magic pills the offending item is now only the size of a pea...........which may mean I can get out of a visit to the dentist whose doors I have not darkened since 1973.....Ii wonder if they still have readers digest in the waiting room!

Hayling Rescue

May 11, 2013

Saturday...midday tide.......

SW 5 to 7 forecast plus strong ebb tide....many incidents... including helping MRSC coming in over the Bar with a fleet of contenders and Finns, and mercifully Katie and Witty are okay after a contretemps with a yacht. Maybe there will be a bit of humour in my next post...

Hayling Rescue

May 11, 2013

You just can't make these stories up....

There we are on the balcony ....not with the Bishop but his chaplain Melvyn Cooper.....watching Blue Moon and Myrtle sailing out of the Harbour in 30 knots gusting 35 knots of breeze....Which is alright unless you happen to be a Wayfarer 3 up intending to sail to the Isle of Wight.......On hitting the rough stuff at the entrance, Blue Moon put in a tack and sailed straight up the beach by Victoria's barrier by Eastoke Point....the other carried on and then Myrtle dropped its mainsail and literally bailed out for the shore....... Hayling Rescue felt it necessary to put in an appearance and escorted Myrtle to Victoria's barrier............. I kid you not Blue Moon and Myrtle were the names displayed on the hulls..........Which reminds me of the old seaside picture postcard which has the two holidaymakers in a passionate clinch in the darkness with a weary looking Melvyn saying ...

"Crickey, you're very amorous tonight Myrtle..."

To which she replies ....

"It's because I am lying on an ants nest!"

Hayling Rescue

May 20, 2013

If you can understand this post then congratulations and tick the tick......

So it's a quiet Saturday afternoon and Hayling Rescue makes the mistake of dismantling the engine cooling water system for a monthly clean ...Cue for voodoophone to come to life ...Sparkes Marina asking HR to nip into Bracklesham Bay to tow in a customer who has seriously damaged his stern gear on a lobster pot.....Seconds later Chi Har patrol is called up by yacht 'Seaweed' wanting a tow back to harbour after jamming his rudder on a lobster pot in Bracklesham Bay...Seconds later fishing vessel 'Seadog' is reporting engine failure in the Emsworth Channel.......So Hayling Rescue quickly reassembles water cooling system and proceeds to Brack Bay to tow in motor boat 'Nautifish'...Hayling Lifeboat is launched to Brack Bay to tow in 'Seaweed' and Chi Har patrol proceeds to 'Seadog' which is put at anchor to await the local SeaStart engineer to effect repair in his motor boat coincidently called 'Seaweed'...........A good time was had by one and all.

Hayling Rescue

May 22, 2013

Tales from an itinerant sea rescuer.......

So there am I sitting in that dentists chair, the first time in 41 years, ready to have that errant molar, which has given me violent headaches for quite a few years.....extracted....When the voodoophone comes to life...........Someone wanting to know when I am having that spooky tooth removed......In goes my first needle injection for 41 years, and then the dentists pliers do their duty and the errant molar is chucked in the bin...and the the the fun begins...The stern faced dentist reads out a list of forbidden things for the next 24 hours....No food, no hot drinks, no exercise, no alcohol, no ... and so on...So the only thing I can do is go and have some sleep and an early night is taken at My Lord's Pond in my warmest sleeping bag. Apart from a territorial dispute at midnight between a seal and a swan, it is a peaceful night followed by a prescribed swill round with water mixed with salt....to be repeated 2 hours later......Will I breach the dentists embargoes?...The Bishop turns up at the club for hot coffee on the balcony.....only to be thwarted by the coffee machine breaking down, at which point the voodoophone comes to life, and the Harbour Office is asking if I will tow in a broken down yacht....I could do with the exercise....So HR proceeds to given position a half mile west of Chi beacon only to find the yacht down by the Langstone Harbour entrance.......And he wants to go to Dell Quay. After the long tow and a nice hot cup of tea, HR returns to HISC to find that the 24 hour embargo has ended, and it is now time to enjoy some of those no nos. I then remembered those parting words from that dentist .....Please do not leave it another 41 years to come back and see us........I may pop in earlier than that if only to finish reading that article I found in the waiting room from the magazine Practical Boat Owner dated May 1999.

Hayling Rescue

May 25, 2013

Probably we all need cheering up, so Tony we need your magic jukebox please....a trio of summer songs...Nat King Cole's ' Lazy Hazy Crazy Days of Summer' and 'That Sunday, That Summer' and finally Mathews Southern Comfort ...'Woodstock' with those wonderful words…

Hayling Rescue

June 5, 2013

Post Script........Call number 5 came late afternoon with a HISC Social Sailor with engine trouble on the way back from Portsmouth..........At this juncture it was thought prudent to relaunch Hayling Rescue a day early.....although the antifouling team from Sparkes warned that the second coat of antifoul needed a bit more than 2 hours to take to the hull..........At least with the boat back in the water it might stem the flow of rescue calls on the jolly old voodoophone...QED.

Hayling Rescue

June 5, 2013

Tuesday Tuesday cant trust that day.......

So we chose Tuesday to crane out Hayling Rescue for its annual inspection, hose off and antifoul new anodes and jet drive unit rebuild.......because Tuesday is the the quietest day of the week......oh no it isn't!!!

At midday voodoophone went berserk with two broken down motor boats in the Hayling area....sorry Sea Start H M Coastguard and stricken yachtsman!!!

Having then hitched a lift to England to buy a new pair of crocs I walked back to HISC...2 hours...only to find a broken down yacht in the Harbour entrance with a flat battery so SeaStart had to come all the way from Lymington to sort out there errant member...sorry Nick...then on Wednesday just before relaunch whilst sitting in the Dentists chair the Harbour Patrol rang to ask if I could tow in a broken down motor boat in the Harbour entrance....sorry Phil.... a very sorry state of affairs......Hayling Rescue is craned out annually and a lot of money is spent on repairs engine servicing new batteries when required and a full tank of diesel every week and then tows in mariners who have not bothered to take the same care........Over to you Tone.

Hayling Rescue

June 6, 2013

Will it ever stop? Post script continued........

So there we were some hours later having coffee with the bishop on the balcony having watched Dave Hollies depart in his yacht on his epic Corporate day....when..................that's right the voodoophone came to life...

"Hello is that the rescue man?".........

"Er... er...yes?"

"I have broken down and on a mud bank between Cockle Rythe and Mengeham Rythe".......

As it was a falling tide muggins departed straight away but it was too late and the motor boat was high and dry on top of a reed bank. The gentleman was told his fortune on the voodoophone link and the intention is to refloat the vessel on the

Friday morning high tide..........voodoophone willing.............very soon Tone Aitken will run out of suitable tunes from his magic jukebox to entertain us. Incidentally the Harbour Patrol had an angler breakdown in his motor launch opposite HISC just an hour earlier.. which makes the grand total of 7 vessels broken down within spitting distance of HISC in just three days.....

Hayling Rescue

June 6, 2013

Post Script to the post script....

Thanks to Ian for bringing back that errant social sailor..........then at 02.30 am. this morning HR was awoken from his nightly tussles with the devil by voodoophone shrieking in the darkness.....

"Good morning."

"Hello Frank can you help us? We have just let go a mooring at HISC to sail to Cherbourg and we have backed on to West Mud and are stuck fast on a falling tide..........."

10 minutes later muggins is on scene and after heeling the yacht over from its masthead spinnaker halyard it springs free and the happy couple sail off to France and muggins returns to My Lord's Pond to continue that nightly contretemps with the devil.........Let us see if Tone can come up with something from his magic juke box...

Hayling Rescue

June 7, 2013

FINALLY and in conclusion the HAYLING TRIANGLE ended its week....I hope.........The gentleman broken down in his motor boat and blown onto a reed back was duly pulled off and towed back to his mooring in blackberry creek...but not without further drama as he fell out of his boat as he picked up his mooring......and HR blocked up its water intakes on a nearby seaweed bank....this was followed by coffee on the balcony with the bishop and Dave Hollies who had a healthy Mushroom Soup...........then the Hayling Triangle spun its web and a motor boat had an engine failure no more than 50 yards from HISC and was drifting out to sea on an 5 knot ebb tide...........Voodoophone saved the day and the vessel was towed to Sparkes...........this made 5 vessels with engine failure within 100 yards of the club in just 5 days........I blame it on Bilderberg Tony.

Hayling Rescue

July 1, 2013

.....Do not leave Sandy Point.....do not leave Sandy Point.....a quiet Monday morning has its uses for muggins to escape to civilization buy some food and sort out the overdraft before the weekend diesel cheque is presented........however just as i leave the grocers voodoophone comes to life.....it is SeaStart the AA of the sea....Can I go and sort out a customer with a Bavaria 35 yacht with a rope around his propeller at Itchenor........? After an unseemly run back to base clutching groceries and various radios muggins goes to sea on HR and is soon on scene at Itchenor with said stricken yacht.Jacques Cousteau does his business with knife to clear errant jib sheet...when coming up for air.....he hears ...the voodoophone shrieking on board HR... It is Sparkes Marina who have a Bavaria 35 yacht sinking on B pontoon...... HR then nips over to Sparkes where the second Bavaria is taken in tow for the crane out berth....HR then returns to Sandy Point where it is decided to use the good services of voodoophone and a friend's online banking system before said diesel cheque rears its ugly head.....clever these Japanese.

Hayling Rescue

July 10, 2013

So after 8 relatively minor incidents in 48 hours I thought I would do another load of drivel with a POST about coffee on the balcony with the Bishop...the voodoophone going berserk etc etc...however the post was too long and the battery on the laptop bblew up and I got distracted by another incident............So we need TONE to play another tune on his magic juke box so how about Harpers Bizarre and 'Feeling Groovy' Tony.....

Hayling Rescue

July 11, 2013

Also Tony I nearly forgot to ask you to put on your magic jukebox 'Schools Out' by Alice Masterman...sorry Cooper.....If it had been released 5 years earlier it would have been my school song instead of 'Lily of Laguna'....thanks Tone.

Hayling Rescue

July 14, 2013

I just knew on Friday afternoon it would be a crazy weekend...........

A mayday call to a vessel with a fire in its engine room meant a high speed dash up to the Chichester channel to evacuate the 15 passengers with the 2 Hayling lifeboats.......apart from a burnt out electric motor all was well.......3 minor incidents on Saturday was followed by a Sunday morning on the balcony without the Bishop who was helping at mattins.......thankfully TONE turned up to sponsor the coffee which when it arrived was closely followed by voodoophone announcing the first of 4 minor incidents in the space of an hour.. I was able to press gang Tony for crew who game fully carried the coffee as we attended the incidents.....He then witnessed Jacques Cousteau in action investigating why a motor cruiser had no drive from his propellor........it had gone ....sheared off together with the shaft ..so no summer holiday in Dartmouth for that unhappy boater...... but all in all no complete disasters although Sunday still has a few hours left.......but at least TONE has some first hand ideas for his magic jukebox response.....thank you Tone.

Hayling Rescue

July 15, 2013

Jacques Cousteau and the ginger nut biscuits.............

As expected Sunday evening was interrupted.......HR was enjoying a packet of ginger nut biscuits and a litre of orange juice (Standard fayre for Sunday Dinner) on the My Lords Pond hideaway when a call came to sort out a yacht off Thorney Island with its anchor and line around its propeller. Jacques Cousteau had to dive down to find a suitable place to tie a second line to existing anchor line and with this done a dive underneath with the bread knife and Jacques was able to cut away the now redundant anchor line twisted several times around the propellor.......as it was a falling tide the yacht was now aground and HR was able to refloat the errant vessel by heeling it over via a masthead halyard and a judicious tug....the yacht then went on its way back to Bosham....On the way home HR came across a becalmed Laser 2000 with 4 people on board and this was towed back to ....Bosham...HR then returned to Fernando's hideaway to finish Sunday Dinner.......a large bar of Cadbury's Fruit and Nut chocolate was a fitting end to a weekend of relatively minor incidemts.....when so much more could have occurred...

Hayling Rescue

July 24, 2013

Carry On On the Balcony......

Readers may be mystified about the plethora of 'Carry On' snippets instead of tales of High Drama on the seas.......It was just that with the absence of high drama....on Monday coffee with the Bishop on the balcony degenerated into a rather pathetic reminisce on the good old carry on films.......as we ended up rolling on the floor remembering such characters as Private Widdle .....the Karsi of Kalibar and the Rumpo Kid......memories of Dr. Moore and Dr. Nookey from the Moore-Nookey sex clinic even brought a smile to the face of the Bishop whilst Tony Aitken (TONE) trawled up more names from Google which even made the lady sitting primly in the corner break into a snigger.........which all goes to prove.....Laughter is the best medicine.....I hope.

Hayling Rescue

July 25, 2013

Carry On Aground...........

"I suppose we are going to be one of your stories on Facebook".....

Said the owner of a yacht high and dry on a sandbank off East Head........his son having anchored said vessel earlier in what he thought was deep enough water......

"I never reveal names " ....I reassured him...I can't pronounce the name of his yacht let alone spell it..............Then I had to tell him it was already all over Facebook via Mark Wood on that club balcony....so Dave Nicholls nee Hollies had picked it up and it was now all over Italy and the Vatican and the World...Colin etc.... .And we had not even begun to refloat the vessel........So I placated the owner by telling him of one of my groundings and if this is time for a confessional I have personally run aground numerous times over the years......Oh Father I have sinned.........Carry On!

Hayling Rescue

July 26, 2013

A right carry on....I forgot to mention the two prime characters in 'Carry on Don't lose your head'....the French Revolution escapade..............Citizen Camembert and Monsieur Bidet.........

Hayling Rescue

July 29, 2013

Carry On Screaming........

Sea Rescue in Chichester Harbour inevitably means mud rescue in obscure places ....The reader will be spared the details, but HR was involved with a potentially serious incident at the very low tide on Saturday morning with 7 horses and assorted grooms and jockeys battling with the sand and mud on the southern edge of Pilsey Sands....Stockers Lake........ then late Sunday afternoon 2 Wayfarer sailors and their boat were discovered upside down with mast stuck in the mud on the south west corner of Thorney Island near Seal Creek..........fortunately all was eventually resolved in both incidents..............So I will carry on screaming .....just.

Hayling Rescue

July 30, 2013

Carry on Jacques.........

So having towed off the Winner Bank a 30 foot motor cruiser aground in a 35 knot squall the skipper was asked where he was going.....

"Littlehampton....."

He replied ....despite my advice to sit out the day in the shelter of Sparkes Marina he carried on outside of the Harbour ..out to sea...at which juncture I voodoophoned HM Coastguard to warn them of the voyage...... 3/4 of an hour later they phoned me back to report the vessel under the tow of the Selsey Lifeboat having picked up a lobster pot with their propeller and now heading for

Sparkes Marina.........Jacques Cousteau was duly summoned and the lobster pot removed via a mask and snorkel dive........The owner is now waiting for a weather window.............Later in the day a MRSC member voodoophoned to report his pride and joy yacht sunk on its mooring in Mengeham Creek.....we will attempt a recovery tomorrow lunchtime.....So watch out for the Epistle to be named 'Carry on Up the Creek'.......Music please Tone...

The Band, 'Up On Cripple Creek'

Hayling Rescue

July 31, 2013

Carry on up the creek.................

HR duly attended the sunken yacht on the Mengeham moorings .....at high tide only the mast was visible but by low tide the yacht was sitting upright in 3 feet of water......the portable electric pumps that HR carries took some 3 hours to clear all the water and the owner found that his cockpit drain pipe had dislodged... hence the quick sinking on Tuesday........ when the tide came back in the yacht lifted on its mud berth and was towed to Wilson's boatyard where it was tractored out into the waiting arms of the insurer's surveyor............the season is over for the owner but at least his pride and joy is repairable and will be spic and span for next seasons sunny weather. A Merry Christmas then to all my readers.

Ian Fiddaman and Frank on patrol.

Hayling Rescue

July 31, 2013

TONE...I was somewhat surprised to see that the most popular item in the recent posts has been the snippet from the cafe scene in 'Carry on Spying'.......it says a lot for the standard of the viewers.....although I am reliably informed the

Bishop resisted the temptation to view the Carry Ons......although the same can not be said for Dave MR Hollies Nicholls.

Hayling Rescue

August 6, 2013

Word has got out that I had my annual day off today....with the Tullochs we visited Diddling Chuch.....Parked on Harting Hill and walked to Beacon Hill fort then had lunch at the Royal Oak Hooksway...the we walked back via North Marden Church..Handle Down...Whitcombe Bottom......Harry completed the assault course but does not want to go again tomorrow Bronwen thinks that Bashall is an honorary Bishop but after all the Carry Ons, Tone's 'All Gas and Gaiters' clip is to be recommended.

Hayling Rescue

August 10, 2013

When the regatta is over..........

HR watchers will have noticed what appears to be white smoke emanating from the exhaust outlet of HR recently. So after the MRSC regatta and the HISC regatta this weekend.....on Monday engineers from Golden Arrow Marine will be dismantling parts of HRS engine to ascertain the fault and effect a repair.....at the moment a hole in the exhaust manifold allowing the cooling water to escape is prime suspect......they will be racing against the clock to finish the repair before Federation Week gets underway....usually my busiest week in terms of the number of rescues..........also as muggins is also in need of a good 2000 hour service I may be able to sneak away for another adventure walk on my beloved South Downs.....So over to TONE and his magic jukebox for 'When the Carnival is over' by The Seekers.

Hayling Rescue

August 12, 2013

Carry On Regardless......

The engineer from Golden Arrow Marine arrives this morning to dismantle the engine Cooling system on HR to try and find the fresh water cooling leak.......A hole in the exhaust system is suspected..........Then major efforts will be made to repair the problem before the start of federation week.........Greg Wells asked the impertinent question

"Why do you always have an engine failure just before Fed Week?".......

The simple answer is that it is near the end of the season and heavy usage takes its toll........HR has attended 125 rescue incidents so far in 2013 and this excessive figure takes its toll on both boat and crew..........therefore muggins will be taking the opportunity to recharge his own batteries ....in the words of the immortal hack....watch this space....

Chet Atkins - 'Engine, Engine Number Nine'.

Hayling Rescue

August 13, 2013

Oh....I nearly forgot to mention the Grumblies.......a dissonant loose group of members who have a coffee with the Bishop on the balcony every Saturday... Chatham House Rules.....during which time most things are discussed and the sinister groups such as the CIA , Mossad , and the General Committee are taken to task....Long Live the Bishop!

Hayling Rescue

August 13, 2013

Carry On up the creek without a paddle....

Golden Arrow Marine duly stripped HRS engine of offending items and duly confirmed that there was a major problem with the exhaust manifold......a replacement has been ordered and a major effort will be underway to put humpty dumpty back together again before the weekend and hopefully before the start of Fed Week........ Once again the financial 'Friends of Hayling Rescue' will access the Very Special Fund set up to pay for the major repair items and as you can imagine a new exhaust manifold plus fitting costs comes to an horrendous sum........ but hopefully HR will be back soon.....thank you friends.....and stand by for the glossary of terms.

Hayling Rescue

August 13, 2013

Glossary of Names....As Bronwen mistook Basher for the Bishop I thought it pertinent to clarify the terminology of the posts.....HR is Muggins..also Jacques Cousteau and of course Frank....Basher is Chris Bashall......The Bishop is Captain Jack Sparrow.....TONE is Tony Aitken...Dave Hollies is Dave Nicholls...Coasties are H.M.Coastguard...Har Pat is the Chichester Harbour Conservancy patrol launch.. the balcony does exist and is at HISC the Financial custodians of the Friends of HR are Chris Driscoll, Nigel Roper, Robert Macdonald, Captain Jack Sparrow and Dave Nicholls, the auctioneer is Dave Spensely Corfield......... and there are many extras who are taking part in the many sagas of HR......Thank you one and all and just just just..........Carry On Regardless.

Malcolm Morley

August 15, 2013

Like a ride on one of the Extreme 40s at the penultimate event in Nice on 3rd to 6th October?

I have the opportunity for one person to ride as 6th man on one of these amazing machines at the Extreme 40 series in Nice in October as well as VIP entry for a partner... and you can raise money for Friends of Hayling Rescue!

I will run it as an auction with the close of auction being midday Thursday 29th August. You can either reply to this post with your bid or message me if you are shy and want to remain anonymous. All money from the winning bid to be donated to Hayling Rescue.

I don't have travel or accommodation included but flights from Gatwick are cheap.

Hopefully it should be a windy event in October! Bidding starts at £50. Please feel free to share this post with your sailing friends if you are not brave enough yourself!

Small Faces - 'Here Come The Nice.'

Hayling Rescue

August 16, 2013

Jacques Cousteau Lives (I hope)...

2 engineers from Golden Arrow Marine spent all day Thursday putting HR's engine back together again....then had to do an oil change and clear up damage from the holed exhaust manifold.. The engine was started up and.......all appears to be okay.....Jacques Cousteau was then able to give it a test up to the Itchenor moorings to mask and snorkel dive on a yacht with a rope around its propeller......so Greg Wells and Robert Macdonald will be delighted and there is a rumour that Peter Hanscombe will be making a very welcome appearance as

crew next week............I wonder therefore what gem Tone will have from his magic Juke box to welcome back HR.......

John Sebastian - 'Welcome Back'

Hayling Rescue

August 21, 2013

CARRY ON OUTSIDE THE FED...............

A lot of rather bizarre incidents around the manor today but only one during the racing.........however TONE has put some rather good bits and pieces together and as well as the humour I do like the Beach Boys, 'We've Been Having Fun All Summer Long'.....I hope

Hayling Rescue

August 22, 2013

Carry On...with the BISHOP..........

The Bishop in his rescue role with the FED kindly rescued a capsized Laser 4000 which had broken rudder pintles. During the hiatus which followed the rudder and assorted bits was lost although the Bishop recorded a GPS position.....of sorts............Muggins therefore was deputised to search for said gear at low tide. Having anchored and swum ashore on the Mill Rythe mudflats Muggins steadfastly wade through knee deep mud and found............nothing. On return to HISC the hose was needed to clear away copious amounts of mud from HR and muggins' wetsuit...at which point the owner appeared and was told of the unsuccessful search on the mudflats...........

"But I did not lose it there, I lost the damn rudder in the main channel......" Wailed the owner.

So we set forth once again to the right target area and found............nothing. Muggins arrived back at HISC and then rushed th Charlie's Farm Store to purchase a delicious supper of a block of cheddar cheese,a big bar of fruit and nut chocolate to be washed down with a cartoon (SIC) of real orange juice......

Hayling Rescue

August 22, 2013

Domestic bliss or domestic Hell.........

A voodoophone call from Sparkes Marina alerted muggins to one of their customers aground outside.....but he did not know where......Muggins duly found the grounded motor cruiser on West Mud virtually high and dry....the customers ...husband and wife, had obviously had something of a tiff as neither appeared on deck to help muggins connect up the tow line...it was too late anyway....eventually the wife appeared and passed a line I connected to a nearby mooring. It was 4 in the afternoon 2 hours left of the ebb and a refloat time of ten at night.......Muggins fell into a deep sleep about nine on the very quiet Mengeham hideaway, and then at ten past ten voodoophone came to life... loudly...

"Hello we've run aground again we've gone about a hundred yards and we've hit another mud bank........"

Muggins arrived about 5 minutes later and towed the subdued couple into Sparkes Marina........But I did detect a more cosy rapport between husband and wife as they safely moored up......Then it was back to muggins' own mooring and in the still of the night muggins could hear very clearly the last 45 mins of the Fed Week festivities at MRSC......somewhat akin to the opening sequence.....fertility dance...of the film ZULU....goodnight.

'Men of Harlech & 'Welsh Anthem' from the Film Zulu.

Hayling Rescue

August 23, 2013

Well when all is said and dine FEDERATION WEEK is over without too many dramas.......

Amazingly four young ladies from HISC and The HOLLIES ran a raffle in aid of the central funding of the Friends of Hayling Rescue which is used for financing the Capital Costs repairs and renewals of the Rescue Boat. A grand total of 171 pounds and 33 pence was raised by Rosie Thompson aged 8...Ella Jones aged 10...Libby Thompson aged 9 and Rosie Prior aged 6......In honour of their grand initiative TONE ...Tony Aitken is putting on a special accompaniment to this post from the jolly old magic juke box...great idea and very many thanks ladies

'Girls, Girls, Girls' Sailor

Hayling Rescue

August 24, 2013

After the Lord Mayors Show.....

Well back to basics and HR was busy Saturday afternoon covering all sorts of Harbour activities...Melvyn Cooper while out coaching spotted an old type INT 14 in trouble on West Mud and called HR on VHF radio to effect a rescue of the vessel which had sprung a leak during the Bosham Regatta. It was towed on its side over the stern of HR to the HISC shore. Countless capsizes were attended but all were able to right unaided......then a Wayfarer with a broken rudder on the Winner Bank was towed back to HISC.......so back to a normal weekend and just who does clear up the poop after that grand procession.......not the Bishop I hope ....over to TONE for another gem.

Hayling Rescue

August 25, 2013

SUNDAY AFTERNOON SYNDROME......

Muggins deals with 20 to 30 rescue incidents every year after club racing has finished. Today there were 4 incidents.....an RS Vision upside down with centre board fallen through and father and daughter sitting on top and thanks are due to Cameron Stewart and Neil Chrismas for helping me right the dinghy and return all to the shore......Then an RS 200 was observed on Stocker Sands continually capsizing and this was eventually righted working my way from the masthead down the shroud to the deck and pulling alongside. It did not help that the helmsman was partially deaf although thankfully I shouted

"DUCK!"

Loudly enough as the boom did an involuntary gybe and missed the helm's head by a whisker. Then a Laser dinghy was reported with a broken mast in the Sparkes Channel and 3 people and their damaged boat were taken ashore to HISC....this was closely followed by a windsurfer with a broken uphaul on West Mud and he was landed ashore.....It only remains for me to request TONE aka Tony Aitken with his magic jukebox to play "Lazing on a Sunday Afternoon' by the Kinks....but I hasten to add if you listen to the words it is not me even if the taxman has taken all my dough..

Hayling Rescue

August 29, 2013

TONE.......we need 'Lightning Strikes' by Lou Christie on your magic juke box.......lightning strikes again again and again.....3 mornings running a yacht up on the Winner Bank......muggins was alerted yet again ...day 3 this morning and although there in less than 5 minutes failed again to get to the yacht before it was standed........Perhaps these yachtsmen are deliberately running aground to avoid going back to work.........I am very wary of the Winner Bank having damaged HR over the years going to the aid of yachts on a falling tide........The stones and rocks do terrible damage powering off the Bank.......still the Lou Christie song is one of my favourites..........play it again Sam no sorry TONE

'Lightnin' Strikes' - Lou Christie

Hayling Rescue

August 30, 2013

Calling out Hayling Rescue does not guarantee being rescued...........

Unfortunately HM Coastguard know I am about early morning, so when voodoophone sprang to life just after 0600 I suspected the worst.... a yacht on the Winner Bank on a falling tide....And would I nip over quick to help him........2 minutes later I was passing my tow line...fearfully aware that often you can end up aground alongside the casualty particularly with the 4 knot ebb willing you to become a fool..... The tow line was fixed muggins pulled clear...just... and then took up the slack in the tow line....then using all the expertise from many years the pull off commenced.................but it was too late....and after a lot of noise and grunt, muggins had to abandon the attempt and left the yacht high and dry on top of the Winner Bank only recently the scene of the Family Fun Week Breakfast........................at least anyway after the Bank Holiday the yachtsman won't have to go to work this morning...........refloat time 1500 this afternoon.....Go for it TONE

Radiohead - High & Dry

HR guides Lady G back to the Pontoon at HISC after a rudder failure.

Hayling Rescue

September 8, 2013

TONE...I already know the magic jukebox accompaniment to this post.............

The weekend was just as bizarre as they always are although Dave Nicholls and his team coped admirably well in the RS Feva grand prix..........afterwards that Sunday afternoon syndrome clicked in and sharp eyed Flo Peters spotted a Topaz dinghy in terrible trouble off the west wittering beach. This was while the peters family were having Sunday roast and father Tim gamefully abandoned his nosh to report the matter to HR who bagged Tim as crew........The intrepid pair found a couple clinging to the sheets of the half capsized dinghy with the mainsail half down....with Trevor Rose reporting the same incident from his lounge......the couple were pulled on board HR, the dinghy then secured alongside and the tow commenced through breaking seas off the shoreline then across the winner bank to the safety of HISC. Other incidents followed and after refueling in Sparkes Marina, Mitch reported Runway racing mark drifting out of the harbour.......this was duly recovered much to the relief of Del Shannon.......

'Runaway' Del Shannon 1962

Hayling Rescue

October 5, 2013

PART ONE of another gripping tale from the high seas.......

Readers will have noticed the lack of dramatic posts in recent weeks........because there have not been any dramas..and so it was on Friday that muggins escaped the confines of the club and made his way to the bank of ponderosa as he was out of cash.......this was fatal as it always is as voodooophone burst into life at said bank.........

"Help I have run aground outside Thornham Marina as the outboard engine on my 19 foot yacht has failed....."

As it was a raging spring ebb tide I had to give the guy the bad news that as he was already aground things could only get worse as I was 40 minutes away...........

Read Part 2 for the gripping sequel.

Hayling Rescue

October 5, 2013

PART TWO of that gripping tale from the high seas ....

So there we were on the Saturday having coffee on the balcony not only with the Bishop but also TONE when.........the voodoophone burst into life again........It was SeaStart asking me to attend a customer in his 40 foot motor cruiser in the Thorney Channel with a mooring buoy rope and chain around his propeller. Jacques Cousteau duly attended the vessel and having dived underneath found the offending items wrapped around rudder and propeller....very nasty........By dint of releasing the strops from the mooring buoy and then deploying trusty bread knife the vessel was cut free to continue his voyage to northney....... Hayling Rescue then proceeded back to HISC only to find a 19 foot yacht with an outboard engine failure drifting onto the Nutbourne Marshes........HR duly went alongside and told the owner that today was a luckier day than yesterday and I would take him in tow to Sparkes...The owner explained that while his engine was new it kept stalling and yesterday he was stranded outside Thornham Marina on a mud bank and had to clamber across the mud to get ashore...........Neither incident was too dramatic but at least these posts confirm that muggins is still alive and kicking and able to have coffee on the balcony........

Hayling Rescue

October 6, 2013

It was now the Sunday in this little sequence and as the Bishop had gone to Winchester for Matins, TONE was kindly sharing the lonely vigil on the balcony for morning coffee......at this juncture obviously voodoophone burst into life...........it was Dave Nicholls, who in a major rescue drama had helped a racing yacht with an engine failure onto an HISC mooring in Selene and would I kindly tow the vessel into Sparkes Marina............the gallant duo thus took to the high seas and did just that when.............voodoophone burst into life.....it was Sea Start and would I kindly put on my bathers and clear the fouled propeller of an 19 foot fishing boat at anchor off the target wreck on the East Pole Sands..............this was duly done and the vessel was able to return to its Emsworth Mooring and Jacques Cousteau returned to HISC to dry his bathers in the warm sunshine............he is now waiting with baited breath to see the magic jukebox accompaniment to this post from the intrepid crewman TONE.......

'Down Down' Status Quo 1974

Colin Ralph

October 20, 2013

Frank. Hope all is well and you got some decent action in during the 'hurricane' or was it tornado. Rosie is an Illex walk resident so hope his place is fine. Question.......what is the name of that cross on the front of your boat I want to do a bit a geeking up on it. Good result for Pompey on Sat. A shame Hearts couldn't even beat the mighty Motherwell!

Frank explains the origin of the Cross Symbol on the bow of Hayling Rescue. "The Fleur-de-Lys Cross represents secrets going back to the beginning of time. The Cross is on Hayling as well as at Rennes-le-Chateau, South of Carcasonne in France."

Peter Walmsley

October 23, 2013

I am continuing to be asked by the gentleman referenced below for direct contact details for Frank Dunster - the email exchanges have gone on since July - first via the Hayling RNLI address and latterly my own. can somebody message me Franks Voodoophone number and I can pass it on... I have removed the email addresses here to avoid them being picked up by Spammers. I know Frank prefers no publicity but this guys seems very keen to thank him personally

Today
Dear Peter,

we have contacted Frank Dunster via his facebook presence, however we got no response. Do you have any further contact details? An address, a phone number, anything would help. I do really appreciate your support regarding this matter!

Thanks,
Thomas

Freundliche Grüße / Regards, Thomas Schoch, Bad Oeynhausen, Germany
Thursday, July 25 2013

Thomas - I should also be clear - Hayling Rescue is a private rescue organisation run by a gentleman called Frank Dunster - Frank was a medal winning helm on the Hayling Lifeboat before he had to retire due to the age limits applied by the RNLI.

22 July 2013
Dear Sir or Madam, on the 9th of July at around 6am we received immense help from 'Hayling Rescue'. We (German sailing yacht Anna, 31 feet) ran aground on Chichester Bar and contacted Solent Coastguard.

Can you relay the contact of the fine Gentleman who pulled us into deep water by attaching one of our halyards to his rib to us, please. Unfortunately we did not get his name, but his call sign was hayling rescue, this is why we believe he was from your Lifeboat Station. I would like to have the opportunity to say THANK YOU to him personally.

Regards from Germany,
Thomas Schoch

Hayling Rescue

November 2, 2013

Saturday was another good day for the sailors! The morning peak gust was 30 knots increasing to 40 knots in the afternoon at Chimet although Cambermet was recording a true 45 knots......so HR had 5 rescue incidents of a mainly minor nature.Firstly an RS Feva sailor got separated from her boat after successfully righting it......then an Int 14 decided to test the conditions and got into trouble on the Winner Bank HR duly attended only to find the errant dinghy blown into the shorebreak off West Wittering beach where HR encouraged the crew to go ashore and avoid further damage.... a long walk back to HISC though.....then a windsurfer's sail would not let him sail home to windward...........immediately followed by Rear Com house and Guy Fawkes reporting an RS 200 in trouble on the Stocker Sands.This vessel with a brand new mast now needed another and it was towed ashore........later a second windsurfer looking remarkably like the first was brought ashore in a 45 knot squall.........but he does have a season ticket.

Hayling Rescue

December 17, 2013

PROVIDENCE........

As you readers are aware odd things are happening all the time around Chichester Harbour and its approaches ...And so it is midday and John Rees has kindly bought the coffee for myself and the Bishop, who has just got back from Winchester..grandson's nativity play....obviously at this juncture voodoophone bursts into life ..it is the harbour master wanting me to tow a disabled yacht into Sparkes Marina from Hayling Bay....duly done and safely in the marina ...the skipper explains he is on his way from Cowes to Rye and his outboard engine fell off crossing a bumpy Hayling Bay...fortunately it stayed connected to the boat via a control cable and complete with transom mounting bracket....and part of the transom.....this voyage has now terminated which is very providential as the coastguard then issued a severe gale warning for tommorrow.......As the very recent weather forecast promised a dry afternoon I stayed in Sparkes to carry out some much needed but routine maintenance on Hayling Rescue.......then it started to rain....heavily.....and my afternoon was now terminated. The number of rescue incidents attended for the year now stands at 185.....will that reach 200 before the year ends...stand by for more gripping adventures.....music please maestro TONE.......maybe something Christmassy like Perry Como's 'Christmas Eve'…

Hayling Rescue

January 1 2014

Statistics damn statistics.......

A quiet new years day enabled me to review the stats for 2013.....186 rescue incidents attended by Hayling Rescue...main category was the 48 boats towed in with engine failure,,,a truly dreadful figure.......25 capsized dinghies righted....27 grounded yachts...another bad feature...Jacques Cousteau dived underneath 13 vessels with fouled propellers.There were 6 broken mast incidents and only 9 windsurfers needed to be brought ashore....The financial friends of Hayling Rescue have been superb potentially raising the bulk of the money needed for new tubes and overhaul for the current boat which has done 14 hard years and 4 hard years since that major engine rebuild of 2010. This will enable me to keep Hayling Rescue running for the foreseeable future..........I am deeply touched and eternally grateful for your overwhelming support.

Hayling Rescue

February 22 2014

A Quiet Saturday afternoon......

Chris Witty had the wits to sail his RS800 back to HISC to report a Moth in trouble with a broken foil north of East Head. HR duly went over to investigate and found the offending Moth on Pilsey Island stripped down and ready to be ferried back to HISC. He had hit an submerged object....foiled again....

We put all the bits on HR and returned to HISC only to find we had left the mast on Pilsey Island....so...returnig some time later. Being a quiet afternoon yours truly went for a walk intending to buy some supper....only for voodoophone to come to life with H.M. Coastguard asking if I would kindly go to East Head and tow a boat with an engine failure back to Chi Yacht basin. The 40 foot yacht had suffered a battery problem so we had to pull the anchor up by hand. The yacht was towed safely back to Chi Marina and HR returned down the Harbour to HISC as dusk reared its head with HR's tummy rumbling.......Thank goodness the Club has a vending machine!

Hayling Rescue

March 4 2014

The Flying Boozer.....

Coffee on the balcony had been a jovial affair with John Rees asking about the merits of commuting to Crawley on a motorbike, the Bishop revealing borrowing his wifes Honda 90 to commute and Giles extolling the virtues of his BMW 1200 with yours truly on train strike days dashing up to work on the BMW R100 RS a match for John's Kawasaki 550 4NFS. Yours truly hated the commute, returning home each day on the flying boozer on account of the dreaded W club.... a drink at every station beginning with a W....

The Bishop intoned like some black mass:
Waterloo...Wandsworth..Wimbledon… Weybridge… Walton… West Byfleet… Woking... Worplesdon… Woking ...Witley....How I hated those days.......

Intuiting that there would be an incident Muggins did some routine maintenance round at Sparkes and then dashing to buy a tin of baked beans for an early supper ....when voodoophone came to life with a request from H.M.Coastguard to help with a tow of a 35 foot motor cruiser struggling against the tide with one engine down and the second a bit dodgy into Chichester Yacht Basin...2 hours later with mission accomplished, muggins came back down the Harbour rejoicing that ho no longer returned home on the flying boozer.......Chi Marina...Itchenor...Cobnor Point...Chalkdock Beacon..Thorney ...East Head...Stocker..Fishery and the HISC Pontoon...Home Safe not a single station beginning with a W and stone cold sober.

'5:15' - Quadrophenia - The Who

A young sailor's broken dinghy saved from the waves.

Hayling Rescue

March 14 2014 at 5:24pm

Oh Father I have sinned or 'Jacques Cousteau lives.......'

It was 0530 in the morning and time for HR to return ashore for morning ablutions.....The mooring at the entrance of My Lord's Pond had been extremely peaceful ...except for the pick up strop with buoy being 4 meters too long........so it got caught around the stern of HR and the underwater exit of the water jet....I would have to dive underneath or cut the line...........after cutting the line I was clear of the mooring ...But where was the pick up buoy? .....Later on I was doing the pre-weekend checks and found the tag end of the strop wrapped neatly around the impeller shaft........so Jacques Cousteau duly dived underneath and pulled clear the strop and an oversized pick up bouy......Having a tinge of conscience muggins returned to the errant mooring and re-fixed the aforementioned items to the mooring....only some 4 meters shorter as it should have been in the first place......Muggins usually averages having to dive under yachts to clear fouled propellers about 20 times a year but never expected the first of 2014 to be his own.......still that early season dive into water of about 9 degrees centigrade did clear that nagging headache.........I hope you all have a good trouble free sailing 2014...

Paul McCartney & Wings 'Jet' 1976

Saw Doctors - Bless Me Father

Hayling Rescue

March 23 2014 at 5:09pm

So this lady at the club reprimanded me for not keeping up a steady stream of posts...... I enjoy a good laugh she said.... I might have one later I replied............So balcony Dave wisely kept the RS Feva Regatta in the harbour...80 boats and race one over the Pilsey Sands and the wind steady at 14 knots.........The VHF radio came to life...there is a squall coming warned Brian C.B......he was right as 40 knots hit the fleet on the downwind leg.....fortunately there was a very good safety team and the fleet was coralled..most bu now upside down.....Dave Nichols gamely abandoned the race and supervised from the Committee boat and Brian C.B. and in particular Chris Bayerman dealt with some serious incidents...Hayling Rescue whilst advising crews to sit on their upside down hulls until the squall passed came across a young lad unable to do this as his drysuit was full of water....he was pulled on board HR and when the squall had passed we righted his dinghy...put him back on board and sent he and his crew ashore.......all the safety crews had done the same when the VHF radio came to life.....Where are the 3 420 class dinghies......out in the Bay......no one answering the support boat's radio....The Marine Manager Mitch was picked up from the pontoon to join he search out to sea and we found the battered 420's on Chi Bar.... one capsized not for the first time as the crew had been trapped underneath during that squall for a short while. HR righted the dinghy via the mast head and with the crew wisely not wanting to sail in any further Mitch gamely transferred to helm the dinghy and the crew was brought ashore....... Then the sun came out and the wind dropped down to 16 knots and then a lot of people went back out sailing............Happy Easter if and when it comes...

Diana Ross - 'Upside Down'

Hayling Rescue

March 30 2014 at 6:11pm

The joys of boating! In quick fire succession the joys of boating presented themselves as firstly a motor cruiser had an engine room overheat and exhaust water box meltdown just passing the RNLI Lifeboat station. The Lifeboat was even afloat nearby and the vessel was towed safely to Sparkes marina where the local fire brigade ascertained that the fire was out. Muggins duly towed the vessel to its home at Emsworth Marina and then returned to Sparkes to refuel only to find a leaking cooling water intake pipe...so the Sparkes Engineer was booked for first thing Monday....then voodoophone came to life and a yacht with an engine failure required a tow on to his mooring up at Sweare deep...this was duly done only for voodoophone coming to life and a yacht requesting a tow off a mudbank between Hayling and Thorney.....Two very novice new to yachting soldiers were found clinging to their newly acquired 20 foot bulb keeled yacht leaning over at a precarious angle.They had already lost their outboard engine when it fell off the Transom bracket......they were towed to deep water and then directed past the navigation marks to the yachts new home on the Thorney Island moorings.......finally muggins returned home to repair the waterproof Echo Sounder which had survived the winter deluges but had given up the ghost now spring had sprung.....fortunately I had a brand new spare.........My two pet hate cliches are 'Have a nice day' and....'Enjoy...'. Over... to you TONE for the music.

The Nice - 'America' 1968

Hayling Rescue

April 1 2014 at 4:58pm

My Day Off...part 2.....

Long suffering readers will recall the attempt to have a day off during each week last year..the experiment being ended at the first attempt by a sinking boat called My Day Off.....So on Monday muggins made another attempt choosing to have today Tuesday for a day off.....Voodoophone sprang to life ...it was Wilson's Boatyard....

"Can you tow a motor boat off the Emsworth moorings and bring it down to us?...So that was Tuesday morning written off and after doing the aforementioned tow down to My Lord's Pond in bright sunshine I was able to have a quick explore of the fabled Grail Creek with the ultra mysterious Pond Head House the home of the author Neville Shute before he escaped to Australia.....the Majestic Mengeham House and the enchanting Tournerbury Woods all surrounding My Lords Pond where I had scattered my Mother's ashes a few years ago.....HR.returned to HISC intending to start my day off early afternoon ...akip in the sun in a quiet corner of the site......only for the club tractor bursting into life nearby to tidy up the car park......I will go for a walk instead........Voodoophone burst into life.....it was a local boatyard...

"We have just launched a Sunseeker powerboat and both engines have overheated down by Mill Rythe buoy can you tow it back for us?.........."

This was duly done and by now it was late afternoon of My Day Off.......Well next week I will try to have Tuesday off again.........Oh bugger.....Next Tuesday I have to renew my First Aid Certificate......Then its Easter and before too long it will be the Moth Worlds then family fun week then Fed Week.......Perhaps I will have My Day Off this year on Christmas Day.... Over to you TONE my music maestro

George Harrison 'My Sweet Lord'

Hayling Rescue

April 4 2014 at 6:53pm

THE GREAT ESCAPE....mark 3........So this twin engined motor cruiser takes a team of post graduate film makers out into Hayling Bay to shoot some water shots for a film about a water-borne escape.

To make it more exciting the camera man in a wet suit takes some shots from the water.....but tethered by a safety line to the boat....except when he is retrieved the safety line gets caught around both propellers and tight on a cleat... The skipper explains his predicament to H.M. Coastguard who agree that he needs some mug to come out to dive underneath to sort it all out......muggins who at this juncture is up at Bosham having towed a newly launched yacht back to its mooring is contacted and proceeds in a southerly direction to said incident.......It being too much swell in the Bay ...banged heads and all that.

 HR tows the vessel to Sparkes Marina where Jacques Cousteau dons his flippers and dives underneath to cut free the errant safety line from the propellers.......what I want to know is, when I saw the film THE GREAT ESCAPE for the second time, why did not Steve McQueen take a longer run up on his motorbike to ensure he cleared that final barbed wire fence?

Mike Sarne 'Just for Kicks'

Hayling Rescue

April 24 2014

Wet Wet Wet.......The Bishop had arrived for coffee on the balcony in a foul mood....Matins had overrun or something, and Brian CB and Dave Hollies were noshows......Then no sooner had we sat down with our daily beverage, the voodoophone came to life........It was a request from the Hayling Lifeboat for Jacques Cousteau to meet them at Sparkes as they were towing in an angling boat with lobster pot lines around its propeller......
The Bishop was informed and told that muggins was about to change into his bathers in order to expedite the request.....the Bishop was not amused to be deserted so soon and rather haughtilly suggested I would need something better than my bathers.......
"I will be wearing a Dry Suit with a wetsuit underneath..." I retorted.............
Which is just as well.....as....making the rendezvous Jacques dived underneath the boat to cut free the line from around the vessels propeller....this took some time...and .....there was the telltale coldness of water permeating the wetsuit, having passed through the drysuit with consummate ease....
With the vessel now free to return to Pompey Harbour muggins suddenly remembered a second motor cruiser in the Marina which also needed Jacques' services having picked up a fishing net on the way back from Cherbourg.......Cousteau dived underneath this vessel and felt another inrush of cold water through the dry suit, this time soaking his bathers as well.......
With the fishing net removed from around the propeller of this vessel, muggins returned to HISC.......to remove drysuit and consign it to the skip.........to bring out the surfer's steamer wet suit for frontline duty.........and to hang up the

bathers in the sun to dry!

Wet Wet Wet - 'With A Little Help From My Friends'

A sailor with a broken collar bone is taken back to shore.

Hayling Rescue

April 26 2014 at 6:28pm

Coffee on the balcony with Brian CB and the Bishop had ended early as there was much sailing going on in the Harbour.....HR was lurking near HISC when voodoophone came to life.....it was Honker from the Lifeboat Station reporting an upside down 420 drifting out towards the Chi Bar.....this was confirmed seconds later when the coach boat requested assistance via VHF radio to the Club...Rory was picked up from the pontoon and HR was soon on the scene.....the crew were safely in the coach boat but the dinghy could not be righted as the spinnaker was jammed from the masthead acting as a deadweight......HR went alongside and Rory grabbed the masthead and the crew were able to undo the spinnaker halyard and the boat was righted by then lifting the masthead upright...the crew climbed back on and sailed home..............however during this manouevre HR's water jet drive lost forward momentum and Rory had to run along the boat from stern to stem still holding the masthead to keep control.........this resulted in the echo sounder breaking its securing bracket.......back at HISC the water jet unit compartment was raised and copious amounts of hydraulic oil had sprayed out from a control hose...................Some 8 years ago Muggins had bought a spare hose and the replacement item was found lurking in a small cupboard...it needed a big pull and it eventually sprung clear pulling out with it 2 spare echo sounder securing brackets................ all were duly fitted...... and HR resumed normal actvities..................NEVER throw anything away you may need it one day....the Searchers TONE....

Searchers - 'Don't Throw Your Love Away'

Hayling Rescue

April 26 2014

On the odd occasion...............Voodoophone had burst into life early in the afternoon..........

"Do you still do rescues?......."

" On the odd occassion" I replied.......

"Well I have run aground on my catamaran and the tide is going out fast.....so fast I can see grass under my portside hull......"

The yachtsman had run aground an hour earlier and had not requested assistance at that juncture.....so Muggins was asked if he would help refloat the vessel at the next tide....midnight.....that would mean I would have to prepare about ten thirty and get back at about 0200 in the morning........not worth going to bed before and not worth going to bed after as i usually awake at 0400.....so I said no but I would help the refloat on the early afternoon tide the next day..................Muggins agonised over the refusal ....and made ready that evening for the refloat arriving just before midnight..the vessel was found still high and dry on a reed bank between West Itchenor and the Chalkdock beacon and the yachtsman was much suprised to see me....!

Sam and Dave - 'Hold On I'm Coming'

Hayling Rescue

May 1st 2014

On the odd occassion....Part 2 of another gripping adventure......

Having beached HR on the edge of the mudbank, Muggins scrambled ashore with the towline and then disappeared down a crack in the hard mud. Trying not to look too foolish Muggins, climbed out and made fast the tow line on the stern of the catamaran........the tide came in ever so slowly and just on High Tide 0115 it was still hard aground......Muggins opened the throttle on HR and ....nothing happened....3 more attempts failed to budge the vessel so full throttle was engaged and ......the catamaran slid off the mudbank and disappeared down the Itchenor Reach at High Speed backwards...Muggins duly caught up and towed the vessel to the nearest mooring advising the owner to stay put for the night and then go back to his mooring in daylight...........HR returned to My Lord's Pond got into the cosy sleeping bag and awoke as usual at 0400.

Hayling Rescue

May 6th 2014 at 5:51pm

With a bit of luck Hayling Rescue will be craned out next Monday May 12 for its annual overhaul at the boat's builder's yard ABC Marine who built the vessel 1999/2000. The Hull will be pressure washed and inspected and certain aluminum repairs will be made. An engineer from Hamilton Water Jet will attend and the water jet unit will be stripped down and rebuilt with the usual 16 anodes renewed. Then 2 coats of antifouling will be applied and after any other necessary repairs the boat should be relaunched on the Wednesday ready for what promises to be a hectic June, July, and August. Then with a bit of luck the boat will come ashore for the inflatable tubes to be replaced after 15 years of abuse and adventure....'Here Comes Summe'r by Jerry Keller appears to be needed TONE

Hayling Rescue
May 10th 2014 at 4:52pm

Ne'er cast a clout until May be out..........SW 35 knots gusting 40 knots with the occasional gust to 45 knots.................Just 5 Windsurfer rescues..............but TONE their theme tune please on your magic jukebox - The Surfaris and WIPEOUT!

The Surfaris performing 'Surfer Joe'

Tracey Covell
May11th 2014 at 10.00

Are you sitting comfortably ? ...It was 35-40 knots, and it was all going so well. I was loving it and thought: "Just one more and in… "

There was no style involved just survival for me at least. So fell off on last run home and could not water start and ended up involved with a large moored yacht (no damage to yacht!). I ended up hanging off the bow of the large yacht and got separated from the board, I got myself onto the mooring line but was behind the big mooring buoy and thought no one could see me. Tide was running and I was quite concerned and very tired trying to hang on.

Of course Frank was watching me and others. It seemed a long time and all the other boards were whizzing past to windward and did not see me. And then out of no where... there was Frank .... the relief was massive. He hauled me in like a whale and I flailed in the bottom of his boat and we rescued the board. My main concern was Sarah Howarth's sail which she lent me….which was fine!

Dinah Washington: 'Mad About The Boy'

Hayling Rescue
May 16th at 1:25pm

My Day Off ..continued...or The Power of Prayer! London Taxi drivers have a charity called the Sunshine Club, and every May they drive 70 kids from deprived homes down to Chi Har for a trip out on a flotilla of boats......one such

vessel had left Sparkes for the Northney Marina pick up point, but the skipper had forgotten to turn the diesel fuel supply tap on and the engine stopped by the Club.....Muggins was duly dispatched to be greeted by the tearful owner not wanting to disappoint the kids.....could I fix the engine?....Muggins is of course the world's worst mechanic and after grabbing a handfull of rusty spanners set to work on bleeding the fuel system through to clear all the resultant air locks.....as usual a spanner slipped off a bleed screw, and blood from Muggins scratched knuckles mixed with dripping diesel fuel.....the system was bled through from fuel tank to the injectors, and the skipper told to press the start switch...........
and..............yes the engine failed to start......the trick with the spanners was tried again and this time ....nothing... then the skippper's radio came to life ..

'Would all skippers please report to trip control for safety briefing.'

At this, skipper looked even more despondent.... Muggins went through the procedure again, and fuel was definitely coming through the injectors So the skipper pressed the start button again....and nothing.....a dispiriting tow back to Sparkes was now in order, but then Muggins called on the Almighty to help in this hour of need.......

'Abracadabra'

Muggins intones as the skipper hits the start button for the last time ......hey presto........nothing....

'Bugger...'

Mutters Muggins, and the engine splutters into life........The boat made the rendezvous, and two happy deprived kids and their chaperon were later seen motoring to East Head for their picnic lunch...

Steve Miller Band: 'Abracadabra'

Hayling Rescue

May 16th 2014 at 1:37pm

My day off continued.....so having had a busy week doing the annual overhaul ....and after the Sunshine Club incident, muggins retired to a much needed coffee on the balcony with Dave Hollies and the Bishop.......You are quite right...Voodoophone did come to life, and Sea Start the AA of the sea wanted muggins to nip out to a boat with a flat battery......On arrival back at the balcony the coffee morning was long over.......Two incidents already, on My proposed Day Off .....What will the afternoon have in store?............Music maestro please TONE

Rolling Stones: 'Start Me Up' Glastonbury 2013

To be continued!

Made in the USA
Charleston, SC
23 May 2014